The 10 Greatest Struggles of Your Life

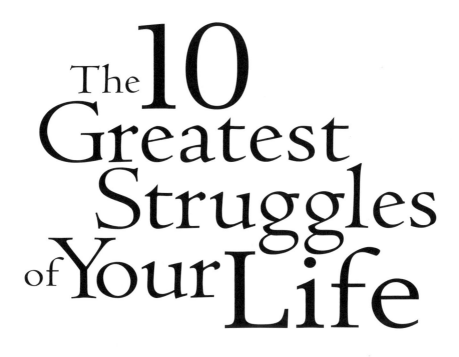

The 10 Greatest Struggles of Your Life

COLIN S. SMITH

MOODY PUBLISHERS
CHICAGO

All Scripture quotations are taken from the *Holy Bible, New International Version*®. NIV®. Copyright © 1973, 1978, 1984 by International Bible Society. Used by permission of Zondervan Publishing House. All rights reserved.

Cover Designer: Smartt Guys Design
Cover Image: Philip and Karen Smith / Getty Images
Editor: Jim Vincent

Library of Congress Cataloging-in-Publication Data

Smith, Colin S., 1958-
    The 10 greatest struggles of your life / Colin S. Smith.
      p. cm.
    ISBN-13: 978-0-8024-6557-3
    ISBN-10: 0-8024-6557-9
      I. Ten commandments—Criticism, interpretation, etc. 2. Christian life—Biblical teaching.
    I. Title: Ten greatest struggles of your life. II. Title.

BV4655.S63 2006
241.5'2--dc22

                                                                            2005030699

We hope you enjoy this book from Moody Publishers. Our goal is to provide high-quality, thought-provoking books and products that connect truth to your real needs and challenges. For more information on other books and products written and produced from a biblical perspective, go to www.moodypublishers.com or write to:

Moody Publishers
820 N. LaSalle Boulevard
Chicago, IL 60610

ISBN: 0-8024-6557-9
ISBN-13: 978-0-8024-6557-3

3 5 7 9 10 8 6 4 2

Printed in the United States of America

For Colin and Brenda,
who know how to prevail
in the challenges of life.

Contents

Introduction

IN CELEBRATION OF HER golden jubilee, Queen Elizabeth II opened the grounds of Buckingham Palace for a concert. The event was a huge success, and ended with a star-studded lineup of musicians including Paul McCartney, Elton John, and a host of others leading a vast crowd in the old Beatles song "All You Need Is Love."

It's a great song, but the words are a long way from the reality of our world, with its war, hatred, and terror, and from our experience of loneliness and fear. Listening to Paul McCartney singing about love, I was struck by the tragic irony that his colleague and cowriter, John Lennon, was gunned down by a deluded fan in a meaningless act of violence.

All you need is love. But how do you find it? All you need is love. But how do you know what love is and where can you hope to find it? God is love, and He calls us to pursue a life that reflects His character. But that's a struggle. In fact, the greatest struggles of our lives revolve around showing love to God and others.

How can we know what God's love is like? The answer is found in the Ten Commandments. They show us what God is like, and they spell out the meaning of love. True love involves faithfulness, truthfulness, trustworthiness, and contentment. These are all dimensions of God's character, and that is why they are the dimension of love.

God is love, and He calls us to pursue a life that reflects His character. That's why He gave us the Ten Commandments. They show us what God is like and spell out the meaning of love. The reason we should not commit adultery is that God is faithful. The reason for not bearing false witness is that God speaks the truth. The reason for not coveting is that God is content in Himself. This is what God is like, and since you were created in His image, this is the life for which you were made.

But this life does not come naturally. The impulses of greed, anger, and self-interest run so deep within us that anyone who seriously tries to live the life described here will soon be convinced that we desperately need help.

To many people, the Ten Commandments are mere relics of history, tablets of stone—valuable perhaps for maintaining law and order in society, but of little use of relevance in everyday life. But the commandments are indeed relevant, and this book will show you how each of God's commands speaks directly to the ten greatest struggles of your life.

God wants to meet with you in these struggles, to teach you the meaning of love and to lead you into healthy, thriving relationships, first with Himself and then with other people in your life.

The accompanying study guide will help you to apply what you learn either in personal study or in a group discussion. I am grateful to my colleague Tim Augustyn for his excellent work in preparing the guide. Tim has a special gift for framing questions that lead you to a deeper grasp of the truth about God and about yourself.

Our prayer is that this exploration of the Ten Commandments will strengthen your faith in Christ and give you great encouragement to press on in the ten greatest struggles of your life.

"YOU SHALL HAVE NO
OTHER GODS BEFORE ME."

◆EXODUS 20:3

Do I love God

unconditionally?

one

Your Struggle
with God

ONE OF THE HOTTEST ISSUES in America today is the debate over values. Our values tell us what is right and wrong and drive us to certain actions. Your personal values can motivate you to donate to a food pantry or make you hide your income from the Internal Revenue Service at tax time. They can cause you to volunteer as a tutor or protect your own self-interests. It's not surprising that teachers, religious leaders, businesspeople, and politicians all agree that our values need to be clear.

Where do you get your values? And how do you know which values are the right ones? Is it all a matter of personal choice? And if so, what are we to say about the values of Hitler, Stalin, or followers of Al Qaeda? They have values too.

Values come from somewhere, and the first thing to grasp about the Ten Commandments is that they reflect the character of God. That's why there is so much controversy about displaying these commandments in public. Secularists object that these commandments are specifically tied to the God of the Bible. And of course they are absolutely right. A different god would have given different commandments.

The God you worship will shape the values you hold, and the values you hold will shape the lifestyle that you choose. The common values that shaped the founding of America arose from a consensus about God. Take away that consensus about God and you lose any hope of consensus about values.

It's not surprising that some people get upset about the phrase "under God" in the Pledge of Allegiance. If we really are one nation under God, that would mean some kind of commitment to live under the values that this God has given us, and that would mean a lifestyle that many people don't want!

Those who choose a lifestyle that differs from the principles of the Ten Commandments need to find a different god, and that is precisely what's happening in our country. When the God of the Bible doesn't fit with where people want to go, they find themselves desperately looking for other gods who will reflect different values, and therefore accommodate a different kind of lifestyle.

A country that chooses to abort forty million babies needs to find a different god.[1] Our society is on a collision course with the God of the Bible, who both gives life and says, "You shall not murder." It's no surprise that the search is on in America for new gods who will reflect our choices.

This attempted reshaping of God is not new. It goes all the way back to the garden of Eden. When Satan tempted the first man and woman, he lured them away from the Lord by suggesting that God's commands were too restrictive.

God had told the first man and woman not to touch the Tree of the Knowledge of Good and Evil. But Satan wanted them to make a different choice. His goal was to change how they behaved. His strategy was to undermine what they believed. "Did God really say that you could not eat from the tree?" he asked. (See Genesis 3:1.) "And this talk about death following sin is surely exaggerated. You shall not surely die. No; on the contrary, you shall be like God. You can be the Lord of your own life. You can decide your own values. You can discover what's right for you!" (See Genesis 3:1–5.)

So Adam and Eve became confused about God. They put themselves in the place of God by grasping what God had not given.

Adam and Eve's first struggle was their struggle with God. They wanted to take God's place, and although the first commandment had not been written at that time, it describes the greatest struggle not only of our first parents, but for all their descendants.

Getting to Know God by Name

"I am the LORD your God."—Exodus 20:2

Throughout history, human beings have made repeated attempts to replace the God of the Bible by inventing other gods that reflected their values. The ancient gods of the Egyptians represented what was important to them: the Nile (the god Osiris), frogs (Hekt), and the sun (Ra). The Babylonians also valued the sun (Bel), but they also placed great importance on wisdom and literature (Nebo), and their city (Marduk). Each of these gods reflected the values of the cultures in which they were created.

In modern times, Communism puts the state in the place of God, capitalism puts money in the place of God, and hedonism puts pleasure in the place of God.

The world has become a marketplace for gods. So the question we have to answer is, "What's unique about the God who gave the Ten Commandments? Why should we follow Him?"

God introduced Himself to Moses at Mount Sinai (also known as Horeb) when He spoke from the burning bush and commissioned Moses to speak to Pharaoh.

Moses wanted to know God's name. That wasn't surprising. Egypt had its own gods, and if Moses said that God had sent him, Pharaoh would want to know which "god" he was talking about.

So God said to Moses, "I AM WHO I AM" (Exodus 3:14).

In the original Hebrew, this was just one word, with the letters YHWH. It's hard to be certain about how this was pronounced, because the Hebrew text of the Old Testament was preserved without vowels.

If you add vowels to YHWH, you could get "YeHoWaH" or in its anglicized form, *Jehovah*, though most scholars today think that the name should be pronounced "YaHWeH."

This is the name by which God made Himself known to His own people. Whenever it is used in the Old Testament, it is translated as LORD with capital letters, and it is surely significant that when Moses brought the newly liberated slaves to Sinai, God used this special name to introduce Himself: "I am Yahweh, (the LORD) your God."

Literally translated, God was saying "I am 'the I AM,' your God." He was saying, "I've got a name. I am not like a lump of clay that you can mold to your own liking. I am who I am. I am your God, and I am inviting you into a personal relationship with Me."

The God of the Bible is who He is. That means He is not whoever you want Him to be. He is neither a product of some ancient culture, nor a reflection of the ideas of Moses. He is who He is.

He is the Creator and the sustainer of all things. He is the unchanging, self-existent God, and that means that He depends on nobody. He is neither helped by our faith nor hindered by our unbelief.

God used the image of a bush that did not burn to make this clear to Moses. Fire can only be sustained as long as it has fuel. But this fire did not depend on the bush for its life. It went on burning, and the bush was not consumed. This was how God made Himself known to Moses. He was saying, "I don't depend on anything or anybody. I exist in the power of My own life. I am who I am."

This sets Yahweh apart from everything else in the universe. Every created thing is dependent. Schools depend on students and teachers. Businesses depend on customers and manufacturers. Churches depend on believers and pastors. Human beings depend on food, air, and water.

But God depends on no one. He exists in the power of His own eternal life. He is God whether we believe in Him or not. Some folks love Him, others hate Him, but none of us can avoid Him. He is who He is. So to make Him your God is to come in line with reality. To resist Him is utter folly.

God's name sets Him apart from all other gods. They were inventions of human history, the products of cultures that sustained them. Like pop stars who rise and fall with the fashion of the times, they rose and fell with the civilizations that shaped them. Nobody worships Bel, Marduk, Baal, or Dagon today. They were designer gods made to fit the demands of a market that has now passed away.

But Yahweh is who He is. He always has been and He always will be. He was not created by our words. He created us by His Word, and that is why it is entirely right for Him to say, "You shall have no other gods before Me."

The Appeal of Unconditional Love
"I am the LORD your God, who brought you out of Egypt,
out of the land of slavery."—verse 2

God could have laid out the Ten Commandments on the authoritative basis of His own divine power. Given who He is, He might have said, "I am your Creator. I made the universe. I have more power than a million nuclear bombs, and so you had better knuckle under and do what I say."

But God does not make His appeal to His people on the basis of raw power, like a dictator. Instead, He says, "I am the LORD your God, *who brought you out of Egypt, out of the land of slavery"* (emphasis added). God has already proved that He is committed to the good of His people, and it is on this basis of His gracious intervention to deliver them from slavery that He appeals to His people to follow His commands.

Life in Egypt had been miserable for these people. Their plight had been hidden, and they had been powerless to do anything about it. They were trapped in a life of poverty, abuse, and oppression with no way out.

Then Yahweh stepped in and brought these desperate people out of Egypt. He rescued them, and now He introduces Himself to them: "I am Yahweh. I am the One who brought you out of Egypt. I sent the plagues on your oppressors. I parted the Red Sea, and I destroyed your enemies. When you cried out, nobody else was listening. But I did. Nobody else cared about you, but I came down to help you. No one else saw a future for you, but I did. I am Yahweh, *your God*, and that is why you must have no other gods before Me."

You will never be ready to embrace God fully until you are convinced that He is good. You may submit to raw power, but you will never love raw power. That's why it is so significant that God invites you into a relationship of love.

Consider the difference between a kidnapper and a lover. A kidnapper may say, "You are mine" on the basis of power. A lover says, "You are mine" on the basis of affection.

Many people have the idea that the Ten Commandments are the talk of an authoritarian deity who, like a kidnapper, is intent on imposing his unattractive will on others. Those who believe this will do everything in their power to get as far away from God as possible.

But Moses and the Israelites knew better. They had experienced the grace of God in their extraordinary escape from slavery, and so they did not hear God's commands as the imposition of an authoritarian deity. They heard the commandments as the intimate talk of a lover who has given everything to win the affection of the loved one, and now embraces her, saying, "You are mine."

The reason you should make Yahweh your God and follow His commands is that He is God and He is good. We see this even more clearly in the New Testament where we discover that the "I AM" took flesh and came to us in the person of Jesus. Jesus Christ is Yahweh (the I AM) with us. That is why He said, "I am the bread of life," "I am the way and the truth and the life," and "Before Abraham was born, I am!" (John 6:35; 14:6; 8:58).

The same God who spoke the Ten Commandments to Moses speaks to us in Jesus Christ, who has come down to bring us a greater deliverance than God's rescue of His people from their Egyptian holocaust. Christ came into the world to set you free from your slavery of sin, death, and hell. Imagine the risen Lord Jesus Christ holding out His nail-pierced hands and saying, "I am the Lord your God. I gave Myself to deliver you. Don't put any other gods before Me." How could you resist such an appeal?

Worship: Cultivating Your Affection for God
"You shall have no other gods before me."—verse 3

God invites you into a relationship of mutual love and loyalty. That's what the first commandment is all about. You can't begin to follow this command until you are persuaded of the love and mercy of God. But for those who believe, the first commandment seems like a natural response of gratitude to the grace of God in Jesus Christ.

Pursuing a life of loving loyalty to God means cultivating your affection for Him. As with any relationship of genuine love, this involves thinking about Him, appreciating Him, honoring Him, desiring Him, fearing Him, trusting Him, hoping in Him, delighting in Him, calling upon Him, and giving thanks to Him.

It means giving God more weight in your life than anything else, so that if you face a decision where every inclination of your heart says no and yet to honor God you would have to say yes, you would say yes—because God carries more weight for you than every other inclination of your heart.

That has been the choice of thousands of believers who have gone to prison and sometimes died rather than renounce the name of Jesus. They are living the first commandment.

As Christians, we gather for worship because we want to cultivate our affection for God. In any relationship, love needs to be renewed and replenished. My love for my wife is renewed as I spend time with her and savor fresh insights into the wonderful person that she is. Fresh love sustains a marriage and keeps a husband or wife from turning to someone else. In a far greater way, it is your enjoyment of God's love and the renewing of your love for Him that will sustain you in following the first commandment.

Repentance: Turning from All That Offends God

Pursuing a life of loving loyalty to Yahweh means turning from all that offends Him. Sins that break the first commandment have one thing in common: They all displace God. When something or someone other than God gains a controlling position in your life, the first commandment is broken, because that position belongs to God alone.

I've found it helpful to identify some of the sins that break the first commandment:

- Pride
- Hero worship
- Infatuations
- Allowing other people to bind your conscience
- Superstition
- Consulting the devil, mediums, or fortune-tellers
- Teaching or believing that all religions lead to God (because it puts all gods on the same level)

Despair is another sin that breaks the first commandment. How can you despair if the Lord is your God? Despair comes when there is something that you want, and your disappointment in not getting it becomes more important than your loyalty to God.

This is a sobering list of sins. I see traces of too many of them in my own life, and they show me how much I still need to grow in learning to love the Lord with all my heart, soul, mind, and strength. Perhaps you feel the same.

The first commandment looks easy from a distance, but once you get up close, you will see how difficult it is. You may well find yourself saying to God, "I can't even keep the first commandment. I am surrounded by other powers that control my life. I need help!"

That's a great way to come to Jesus. Following the first commandment is a lifelong struggle, but with the help and presence of Christ you can begin to pursue it.

The Foundation of Freedom

The first commandment brings many wonderful blessings for those who follow its path. Making the Lord your God will deliver you from the grip of forces that might otherwise dominate your life.

I have often spoken with people whose lives were dominated by an overbearing parent, an authoritarian pastor, or a manipulative friend. In these dysfunctional relationships, somebody else has been assuming the place that belongs to God.

God wants to deliver you from all these forms of oppression. He makes this clear in the first commandment, "You shall have no other gods before me." That's liberating! Keeping the first commandment will deliver you from infatuations with other people and from the domination that others may seek to exercise over you.

The first commandment is the basis of our rejection of tyranny: "No other gods before Me!" That leaves no room for dictatorships. No man has the right to assert himself in the place of God.

The first commandment lays the foundation for freedom. It is no accident that free countries around the world have, at least in their heritage, honored the Ten Commandments. So it is a great tragedy that many in America today want to move away from these commands.

A house cannot stand if its foundations are undermined. Those who reject the Ten Commandments in the name of freedom will find at length that the freedom they seek is lost because the foundation on which it rests has been destroyed.

The First Love of Your Life

It's worth considering what other gods we might be tempted to put before Yahweh today. Noting that God is a trinity of persons, Bible scholar James Packer suggests some other trinities that vie to take His place: sex, shekels, and stomach; pleasure, possessions, and position; football, the firm, and the family.

All of these are good gifts from God. But any of these can become an area of sin against the first commandment if the specific gift becomes more important to us than the Giver. That is idolatry.

What dominates your thoughts, your goals, your conversation? What is the first love of your life? That is your god.

Commitment: Embracing the Lord Unconditionally

In the first commandment, Yahweh is inviting you to take a step of faith in which you embrace Him unconditionally as your God. He invites you to do this on the basis of trust, knowing that He is God and He is good.

His appeal is made on the basis of love. He is the God who has come down in Christ to deliver you from sin, death, and hell and has done this by laying down His own life on the cross, and then rising again to make a way through death and into everlasting life for you. He offers Himself unconditionally to you and invites you to offer yourself unconditionally to Him.

It's rather like the marriage service: God invites you to take Him as your God for better, for worse; for richer, for poorer; in sickness and in health, forsaking all others, and keeping only to Him until death brings you into His presence. Making this kind of commitment to God is a wonderful foundation for marriage. Indeed, if you can't make this kind of unconditional commitment to God, how can you hope to make such a commitment to someone else?

Folks who want to negotiate with God usually want to negotiate with everyone else as well. But when you have grasped the unswerving strength of God's self-giving love for you, and you have offered yourself fully to Him, you will begin to discover what a lifelong unconditional covenant of love looks like, and that will help you to offer such love to someone else.

Killing the Conditions

Your challenge is to embrace God unconditionally. The first commandment leaves no room for an "if," "but," or "when," because as soon as you say "if," "but," or "when," you have put something else in the place of God and thereby broken the first commandment.

If you say yes to God but then add, "*if* you give me my health," or "*if* you bless my family," or "*if* you solve this problem," then you are putting your health, God's blessing on your family, or the resolution of a problem in the place of God.

The first commandment is our greatest struggle because we always want to set conditions. We want to use God instead of letting Him be God. But as soon as you try to use God, you have taken Him off the throne of your life and put whatever use you have for Him there instead.

When Jesus said, "Follow Me," His disciples did not know where He would lead them, and you can't know that either. Making Christ

Lord of your life could get you into some tough situations. The nine commandments that follow describe the life God is calling you to lead. Every one of them will be a struggle. But God is calling you to take a step of commitment based on trust, because you know that He is God and that He is good.

Are you ready to embrace the Lord as your God unconditionally?

Note

1. Since the 1973 Supreme Court decision (*Rowe v. Wade*) to legalize abortions in America, more than 1.2 million babies have been aborted every year.

> "YOU SHALL NOT MAKE FOR
> YOURSELF AN IDOL."
>
> ◆EXODUS 20:4

Am I worshiping

God as He is?

two

Your Struggle
with Worship

AFTER A RECENT CHURCH SERVICE, a middle-aged couple greeted me and said they were visiting for the first time. They had heard me speak on the radio and decided that they would come to check out the church.

After introducing themselves and commenting on the radio program, they said, "You don't look anything like we imagined." That got me wondering what they were expecting! I was tempted to ask but decided not to pursue that track in case I had been a big disappointment!

It is natural for our imagination to create an image of something or someone we have not seen. And since God is invisible, it is natural for us to create within our minds, or in art and sculpture, images that are intended to represent Him.

The problem with these images is that they cannot capture the glory of the Creator. All they can do is diminish Him, and that is why God tells us in this second commandment that we are not to make any images that are intended to represent Him.

Some people say that they find icons, beads, or pictures of Jesus to be helpful aids to devotion. But we should not try to be wiser than God. An image or icon may reflect part of the truth about God, but it will always obscure as much as it reveals. Our second great struggle is to properly worship our God, the majestic Creator and Lord, without diminishing Him to a little god.

Take Michelangelo's famous painting on the ceiling of the Sistine Chapel, *The Creation of Adam,* in which the finger of God reaches down to touch man. The painting communicates God's power, but it completely obscures His love. Nobody who looks at that picture could ever conclude that God is full of compassion.

Pictures of Jesus in children's books usually have the opposite effect, giving the impression that Christ is weak, supine, and anemic.

Many people wear or carry a crucifix showing an image of Jesus hanging on the cross. It shows that Jesus died for us, but it completely obscures the truth that He is no longer on the cross, that He has triumphed over death and is seated at the right hand of the Father in glory.

Art and sculpture are wonderful gifts that can be used to capture the beauty and wonder of created things, but they cannot capture the glory of the Creator. Though they may appear to enhance our worship, their true effect can only be to diminish our thoughts about God.

At first sight this second commandment looks easy. Right now, you're probably not struggling with an overwhelming temptation to rush into the garage and shape a piece of wood to be used as an object of worship. But the second commandment goes deeper than issues of icons, art, and sculpture. God is so great that even our best thoughts about Him fall far short of grasping His glory. That's why worship is the second great struggle of your life.

God is greater than your highest thought about Him. You cannot reduce Him to a system of logical thought. You cannot confine Him to the narrow boundaries of your experience. Nothing in creation can represent the Creator. "To whom will you compare me or count me equal?" God asks His people, "To whom will you liken me that we may be compared?" (Isaiah 46:5).

God's love for you is far more than the deepest and most intimate love you have ever known. His power is far greater than any force you have ever encountered.

We cannot find Him or know Him through a self-initiated spiritual search, but God has made Himself known in the Scriptures and has come near to us in Jesus Christ. We know Him not by cultivating our imagination, but by believing His revelation.

Loving God As He Is

In the first commandment, God calls us to embrace Him unconditionally. In the second commandment, God calls us to embrace Him as He is.

God is not like a lump of clay that we can shape into any form that is pleasing to us. God is who He is. He is a person to be loved and worshiped, not a resource to be used.

In his book *The Screwtape Letters,* C. S. Lewis points out that one of Satan's master strategies is to keep us from noticing the very different ways in which we use the word "my" when we speak about "my boots," "my dog," "my wife," "my country," and "my God."[1]

The interesting thing about these five expressions is that they span the spectrum of love. My wife, Karen, recently bought a new pair of shoes. She finds them really comfortable and told me that she "loved" her new shoes. Later in the same day she said that she "loved" me. I hope there is some distinction in the way the word *love* was being used!

The five statements, "my boots," "my dog," "my wife," "my country," and "my God," take us all the way from ownership to worship. They move from things that are to be used to the One who is to be worshiped. Let's take a closer look at the spectrum and face the challenge of where you are placing God on it.

My Boots: I choose my boots because I like the way that they look, because they fit my style, and because they are comfortable for me to wear. My boots exist entirely for my comfort, use, and pleasure. If I tire of my boots, or if they wear out, I can replace them. My boots help me avoid pain, but if they ever give me pain, I will dispose of them instantly.

My Dog: A dog can be very useful. It can be a good friend and good company. A dog can guard your property and help you to get some exercise. There are all kinds of uses for a dog, but a man who treats a dog in the same way as he treats his boots would be a disgrace. A man may own a dog, but if he does, he is responsible for that dog. A relationship of loyalty is involved here. The dog is more than the boots.

My Wife: A man who cannot tell the difference between "my wife" and "my boots" is in serious trouble. And yet, the tragedy of some marriages is that a relationship in which God intends a husband and wife to share mutual love and support can easily degenerate into an arrangement of mutual convenience in which two people fulfill certain functions for each other.

Revisiting the description of "my boots" and relating these words to marriage, we get a painfully familiar picture of a dysfunctional relationship: "I choose my wife because I like the way that she looks, because she fits my style, and because she is comfortable for me to be with. My wife exists entirely for my comfort, use, and pleasure. If I tire of my wife, or if she wears out, I can replace her. My wife helps me avoid pain, but if she ever causes me pain, I will dispose of her instantly."

My Country: Here we move even further away from ownership in the direction of being owned. I do not own my country. My country is far bigger than I am, and I owe loyalty to the country to which I belong. There may be a time when I am called upon to lay down my life for my country. In the great words of President John Kennedy, I am not to ask what my country can do for me; I am to ask what I can do for my country.

My God: Here we come to a relationship of worship in its purest form. But here's the problem: Some folks can't tell the difference between "my God" and "my boots."

Saint Augustine defined idolatry as worshiping what should be used or using what should be worshiped. Idolatry confuses the Creator with the creation and regards Yahweh, the One who is to be worshiped, as a resource that exists for our convenience and pleasure.

Grasping this has helped me to see that idolatry comes much closer to home than carved statues of wood and stone. Idolatry involves putting the things we love in the place of God or seeing God as a means of getting the things that we want, and that's the second great struggle of our lives.

Worshiping What Should Be Used

Idolatry takes a thing that is to be used and puts it in the place of the One who is to be worshiped. It might be my car, my house, my music, my career, my sports, my sexuality, my money, my family, or my country. All of these are good gifts from God, but when created things take the place of the Creator, they become idols.

The way to dethrone created things that could become idols is to ask what they are for. Take marriage, for example. Whether you are married or not, this wonderful gift from God can easily become an idol. Once you see that marriage is a relationship in which God calls you to serve Him, it will save you from making an idol of your marriage or your desire to be married.

Families can become idols if we forget what they are for. Children are a gift from God, entrusted to parents as stewards who are to raise them for His glory. Seeing God's purpose in giving children will save you from making an idol of your children or your desire to have a family.

The same principle applies to your money, which is also a resource to be used wisely for God's glory. Seeing this will save you from making an idol of the money you spend or save.

Most important, you need to know what your own life is for. You are not a machine that exists for production or a soul that exists for pleasure. You are a special creation of Yahweh made in His image and for His glory. That's why the way to find and fulfill your purpose is to become a worshiper of Him.

Take a few moments to ponder this question: Has what you do for God become more important to you than the Lord Himself? That's idolatry: worshiping what should be used.

Using What Should Be Worshiped

The second dimension to idolatry is attempting to use the One who should be worshiped. When Yahweh invites us into a relationship with Him, the instinctive response of our fallen nature is to think that a relationship with God could be very useful.

After all, God is very powerful, so think what He could do for us. We could ask Him to protect our country, give us health and prosperity, bless our families, grow our church, and generally make our lives wonderful. So we come to think of God like Aladdin's genie, an excellent way of getting what we want, and that is idolatry.

Something within me wants to use God more than I want to worship Him. I want Him to forgive my sins. I want Him to get me into heaven. I want Him to give me good health, long life, an intimate marriage, success in my career, healthy children, and multiple grandchildren. The list is unending, and if I find that I go without one of these things, I am tempted to find fault with God.

We are never in more danger of seeing God as a resource to be used than when we come to Him in prayer. Somewhere deep within our hearts lurks the idea that if God really loves us, He is under an obligation to give what we ask and that if we ask in faith, He really owes it to us to come through. That's idolatry. Prayer is not a tool for manipulating God. True prayer is offered in the name of Jesus Christ, and that means that it can only be offered in submission to His will.

Writing on this second commandment, David Field says, "The explosive power of the living God cannot be harnessed. He is never at our disposal. We cannot bargain with him. He is there to be worshiped, not to be manipulated."[2] Idolatry attempts to put God at my disposal. Worship is putting myself at the disposal of God.

Why Idols Are Offensive

"You shall not bow down to [idols] or worship them; for I, the LORD your God, am a jealous God."—Exodus 20:5

Notice that the word LORD is printed with capital letters. God is using the name *Yahweh,* which means "I am who I am." Literally translated, God said, "You shall not bow down to [the idols] or worship them, for 'I am who I am.'"

The reason God gives for not bowing down to idols is that He is who He is, and He does not want you or me pretending that He is whatever we want Him to be. That would be deeply offensive.

This is a message that our postmodern culture desperately needs to hear. God is not whoever we want Him to be. He is not a projection of our latest trends or aspirations. He cannot be reshaped according to our convenience or comfort. God is who He is and that's why we are not to make idols by projecting our own ideas and desires onto Him.

The Ten Commandments spell out the full meaning of love. As we will see, the first four commandments show what it means to love God, and the last six lay out what it means to love your neighbor. Love accepts and embraces people as they are. Attempting to reshape a person to suit your fantasy is just about the most offensive thing that you could do.

Imagine the scene in a candlelit restaurant as Harold proposes to Heather. Stooping to one knee, he reaches into his pocket, produces a ring, and says, "Heather, will you marry me? You are not really what I am looking for, but I think that you have potential. I'd like you to lose a little weight. I need you to change your entire wardrobe, and the strange way that you laugh really irritates me. Also, you need to do something about your strange accent, but I want you to know that I love you."

Harold's words are utterly offensive. Most likely, Heather will rise up, slap Harold across the face, and say, "You don't love me at all. You are in love with an image that only exists in your mind. I cannot be your fantasy. I am who I am!"

Imagine God saying that to you. God is not some impersonal spiritual force that exists to fulfill your fantasy. He is who He is, and any attempt to make Him conform to what we want Him to be is utterly offensive. Loving God means embracing Him as He is.

The second commandment is a good test of your response to the first commandment. If the God you believe in has been shaped for your own convenience, you have not made Yahweh your God, but have put another god of your own making before Him.

In our postmodern culture, many people feel that the diverse religions of the world show that men and women are seeking after God across the entire breadth of the human race. But the Bible regards idolatry not as an expression of our seeking God but as an evidence of our rebellion against Him.

Embracing God unconditionally (the first commandment) means embracing Him as He is (the second commandment). If the god you worship is a god of your own making, you are not worshiping Yahweh, but a collection of your own ideas. You have put yourself in the place of God. That's the offense of idolatry.

Why Idols Are Useless

The idea of inventing your own god or becoming your own god seems very attractive, but the reality is that a god created by you exists only in your imagination, and a god who exists only in your imagination is useless.

The twentieth century in America saw the attempted dethroning of God and the enthroning of the individual in our society. We put ourselves in the place of God. Imagining ourselves on the throne, our statements of faith have lost their meaning. "In God we trust" has become "We trust in ourselves." "One nation under God" has become "One nation pleasing ourselves," and "God bless America" has become "Let's all bless ourselves." But having put ourselves in the place of God, we are left with no place to turn in times of trouble. We are alone with no hope or help beyond ourselves.

The actress Shirley MacLaine expressed most clearly her own attempt to fill the place of God in these words: "I know that I exist, therefore I am. I know that the God-source exists. Therefore It is. Since I am a part of that force, then I am that I am."[3]

If Shirley is the "I am," I feel sorry for the rest of us. And I feel sorry for Shirley. Who can she turn to?

In contrast to the loneliness, isolation, and ultimate futility of having no one to turn to beyond yourself, the Bible tells us about the living God who came into the world in Jesus Christ so that you could know Him and share in the triumph of His risen life forever.

The comfort of knowing and belonging to Christ is beautifully expressed in the Heidelberg Catechism, which is a marvelous statement of the Christian faith set out in the form of questions and answers. The first question and answer are as follows:

Q. *"What is your only comfort in life and in death?"*
A. *"That I am not my own, but belong body and soul, in life and in death to my faithful Savior Jesus Christ."*

God's Image in Christ

The reason God places such importance on us not making images to represent Him is that nothing should detract from the one true image of God that we have in Jesus Christ.

God jealously excludes every other image because it is through the one true image that He has made Himself known. God has taken human flesh and entered the world, making Himself known in Jesus Christ. Jesus is the one true image of the invisible God. He is the exact representation of God's being (Colossians 1:15; Hebrews 1:3). That is why Jesus could say, "Anyone who has seen me has seen the Father" (John 14:9).

You won't find your way to God through an idol. Nothing created can lead you to the Creator. But you can come to God through Jesus, in whom God has drawn near to you. If you will embrace Him, He will embrace you, and that is where eternal life begins.

Declaring the One True God

The challenge to embrace the one true God is made more difficult in a society where some political and religious leaders want the name of Jesus silenced in public. Christians are being told to let people embrace God any way they wish—not as He is. "If you believe Jesus is God's Son, that's OK, but keep the idea to yourself."

Are you willing to believe Jesus is God in the flesh and declare Christ as the only way to God? Then expect opposition on earth. A Connecticut pastor recently began a town council meeting with prayer, ending the invocation with "in Jesus' name." Days later, several clergy met with him, asking that he not speak the name of Jesus publicly again. "When he explained that he couldn't do that, they proceeded to take out ad space in the newspaper, calling him 'divisive,' isolating him from the religious community of his town."[4]

Pastor Joseph Stowell once attended the Chicago Leadership

Prayer Breakfast, where he listened to four members of the clergy (a Jewish rabbi, a Catholic priest, a Protestant pastor, and an Islamic cleric) lead prayers just two months after the terrorists' attacks on New York and the Pentagon. None of them used the name of Jesus. "No one said that He wasn't welcome, but the message was clear. All our 'gods' are to be equal."[5]

The rector of New York's Trinity Church was the keynote speaker. He gave heartrending stories of tragedy and triumph at Ground Zero—and then he called on the audience of clergy and governmental leaders to give up the "traditions that divide those of us who believe in God."

His message to embrace all beliefs in God—and thus redefine God "as you like Him"—received a standing ovation. Stowell, along with some Christian friends scattered throughout the room, remained seated as the applause rolled over them. No doubt some of the audience stared in disbelief, and perhaps embarrassment, at those seated.[6]

Let God be the "I am who I am," and some will call you intolerant, arrogant, or even a bigot. But others will consider the words of Christ and because of your declaration and the Spirit's power believe the no-holds-barred words of Jesus: "I am the way and the truth and the life. No one comes to the Father except through me" (John 14:6). No matter people's responses, we are to honor the name of the one true God.

Notes

1. C. S. Lewis, *The Screwtape Letters* (Glasgow: Collins, 1955), 109.

2. David Field, *God's Good Life* (Leicester, England: InterVarsity, 1992), 72.

3. Brian Edwards, *The Ten Commandments for Today* (Bromley, England: Day One, 1996), 79.

4. Joseph M. Stowell, *The Trouble with Jesus* (Chicago: Moody, 2003), 25.

5. Ibid., 14.

6. Ibid., 15, 22–23.

"YOU SHALL NOT MISUSE THE
NAME OF THE LORD YOUR
GOD, FOR THE LORD WILL NOT
HOLD ANYONE GUILTLESS WHO
MISUSES HIS NAME."

◆EXODUS 20:7

Am I trying to

manipulate God?

three

Your Struggle
with Religion

THE WAY YOU USE a person's name says a great deal about what you think of them, and the way that we use God's name is one of the clearest reflections of His reputation in our culture.

This came home to me when I looked up the name *Jesus* in my *Concise Oxford English Dictionary.* Two definitions are given as follows. Notice the order in which they occur.

> **Jesus:** (vulg.) excl. expr. surprise, impatience, etc. [2] name of founder of Christian religion *d. c.* A.D. 30

The *Concise Oxford English Dictionary* tells us that the name *Jesus* is first a vulgarity. It is an exclamation expressing surprise or impatience. According to the *Oxford English Dictionary,* that is its most common use, though the name *Jesus* can also refer to the founder of Christianity who died around the year A.D. 30.

It shouldn't surprise us that those who do not know the Lord should use His name as an expletive. But too often, the same pattern of speech is found among believers.

The challenge of honoring the Lord in a world that misuses His name begins early in life. I encourage Christian students in middle schools and high schools to tune in and listen to how often the name "God" is misused in one day. Just listen. It will astonish you. You are surrounded by the misuse of God's name. It is natural to people who don't know God, but not for you.

If you have gotten into the pattern of saying "Oh my God," or "good God," or "Oh God" every time you are surprised, ask for God's help to overcome that habit, and ask a good friend to hold you accountable as you make the change.

Swearing is a significant issue, but it hardly seems to qualify as one of the ten greatest struggles of our lives. But the third commandment is about much more than swearing. In fact, as we will soon see, it speaks directly to one of the world's greatest struggles today.

Distorted Claims

Our advertising and marketing culture places great value on endorsements. Celebrities are paid large amounts of money for the use of their names, and we have become familiar with commercials that associate well-known personalities with products. Advertisers use celebrities because big names cause people to sit up and take notice. The endorsement of a big name can put you on the road to success.

No name in the universe is bigger than the name of almighty God, so it is not surprising that throughout the history of this world, people have rushed to attach God's name to their particular cause and to claim His endorsement for what they do.

The name of God has been attached to some of the most hor-

rific acts of violence in our time. We live in a world where some people will fly planes into tall buildings claiming that they do it in the
name of God. Others will volunteer to strap explosives to their bodies and walk into a crowded street with the aim of destroying themselves and as many other people as possible, again claiming that they
do this in the name of God.

It's easy to point the finger at Muslim extremists today, but you
only have to read Christian history to realize that the problem comes
closer to home. Western history is littered with acts of violence that
were done in the name of God. Perhaps the most notorious were the
Crusades, where thousands of Muslims were slaughtered by Euro-
peans who fought under a banner bearing the emblem of the cross.

So it is hardly surprising that many people, noticing that a great
deal of violence in the world seems to be associated with the name
of God, have concluded that His name is a liability.

The government in France ran into a storm of protest recently when
leaders proposed legislation that would ban the wearing of religious head
coverings in schools. Their proposal was based on the premise that France
is a secular republic, and the assumption seemed to be that since God's
name would disrupt social harmony, matters of faith should be kept in
the private sphere and not indicated in any open or public way.

This sad situation is one result of the misuse of God's name on a
massive scale. No name has ever been misused more than the name of
God, and the result is that millions of people struggle over the very
mention of His name. The misuse of God's name lies behind the
most urgent issue in our world today. That's the relevance of the third
commandment.

Conflicting Claims

The name of God is used in support of claims that are so obviously contradictory that a growing number of people have given up
hope of knowing any truth about God at all.

The movie *Vertical Limit* tells the story of a group of mountaineers who attempt to climb K2, the world's second-tallest mountain peak. An avalanche buries three of the climbers, and a quickly assembled team undertakes a rescue mission.

The rescuers are regularly in danger of losing their lives. At one point when two members of the rescue team stop to rest, the conversation turns serious. Kareem, who is a Muslim, lays his mat on the snow and kneels down to pray. His climbing partner, who doesn't have any kind of faith, is taken by surprise, and asks, "Do you believe in hell, Kareem? Do Muslims believe in hell?"

Kareem tells him that they do.

"You're all the same, your lot," his friend says. "Born-agains say if I don't believe in Jesus, I'll go to hell. Jews say if I do believe in Jesus, I'll go to hell. Catholics say if I don't believe in the Pope, I'll go to hell."

Any way you look at it, Kareem's friend seemed to be in trouble.

In a world of conflicting claims that all use the name of God, many people are saying, "They can't all be right, and maybe none of them are right, so I will go with what suits me."

This was Pilate's problem. The Jewish leaders said that Jesus had committed blasphemy against God because He claimed He was the Son of God. Pilate was a Roman politician, and he concluded that on an issue like this, there was simply no way of knowing who was right. "What is truth?" he asked (John 18:38).

Good question. What is an ordinary person to make of the many conflicting claims that all assume the endorsement of God's name? How do you know who you should believe, if, indeed, you should believe anybody? There is no way to answer this question unless there is one God who has made Himself known, and that is precisely the claim of the Bible.

Empty and Frivolous Claims

Misusing God's name is also an issue within the church. Enormous damage has been done to the cause of Christ by the actions of pedophile priests who carried the name of God and yet brought such pain and devastation to vulnerable lives.

Sadly, the highly publicized cases of misusing God's name are too often mirrored in Protestant churches where leaders behave in ways that make the name of Christ profoundly unattractive to many.

Too often, God's name has been attached to false promises of health and wealth, or a fulfilling and satisfying life. The gospel has been repackaged and marketed in a shameless appeal to our arrogance and self-centeredness, with the result that a growing number of younger people have concluded that Christianity is simply too selfish to be true.

Then there is the problem of the frivolous use of God's name. Nobody has described this problem better than Bible scholar David Wells. "One of the defining marks of our time," he says, "[is] that God is now weightless. . . . He rests upon the world so inconsequentially as not to be noticeable."

Wells adds: "Those who assure the pollsters of their belief in God's existence may nonetheless consider Him less interesting than television, His commands less authoritative than their appetites for affluence and influence, His judgment no more awe-inspiring than the evening news, and His truth less compelling than the advertiser's sweet fog of flattery and lies."[1]

If God's name does not carry weight in the lives of Christians who profess to love Him, how will He ever carry weight in the lives of those who do not?

Presumptuous Claims

The most common misuse of God's name among evangelical believers is the presumptuous way in which we often claim God's direct guidance by announcing that "the Lord led me," or "the Lord told me."

Let's take a moment to ponder what that means. God can do

whatever He chooses, and I have no doubt that He is able to speak directly as He did to the apostle Paul on the road to Damascus. But that is not His usual way of operating, so we should be very careful about using God's name as an endorsement for our own ideas that could in time turn out to be a mistake.

Claims that suggest a direct hotline to heaven, in which the Almighty personally directs you in such a way that you know the mind of God beyond all shadow of doubt, are presumptuous.

They leave no room for testing what you believe God has said, and no place for listening to other believers who also have the Holy Spirit. The use of God's name by spiritual leaders to endorse their own ideas is manipulative and can become a form of spiritual blackmail. It is an offense to God and a sin that He does not take lightly.

Those who seek to follow Christ will pray about their decisions and try to apply the principles of Scripture to the choices they need to make. Knowing that the Holy Spirit lives within us, we will seek to discern what is best (Philippians 1:10), and we believe that the Lord is able to give that discernment.

But surely it is more honoring to Christ and more fitting to the spirit of humility to say, "I *believe* that the Lord has led me" or, "I *feel* that the Lord has directed me," when describing our experience of guidance.

God Takes It Personally

If you have struggled because of the way that God's name is repeatedly misused in the church and in the world today, you need to know that this is also an offense to God. How would you feel if someone used your name to promote acts of violence, empty promises, or frivolous ideas? God takes this sin personally. You would do the same.

God will not associate Himself with those who misuse His name. Speaking through the prophet Jeremiah, God said, "The prophets are prophesying lies in my name. I have not sent them or appointed them or spoken to them. They are prophesying to you false visions, divinations, idolatries and the delusions of their own minds" (Jeremiah 14:14).

Jesus also spoke about how on the last day He would publicly and permanently disassociate Himself from those who misused His name.

> "Not everyone who says to me, 'Lord, Lord,' will enter the kingdom of heaven, but only he who does the will of my Father who is in heaven. Many will say to me on that day, 'Lord, Lord, did we not prophesy in your name, and in your name drive out demons and perform many miracles?' Then I will tell them plainly, 'I never knew you. Away from me, you evildoers!'" (Matthew 7:21–23)

Notice how Jesus indicates that *many* people will use His name for their own ends, and that on the last day, He will disown them.

Opening a Franchise

The way that a franchise business works can help us to understand the offense involved in misusing a name. If you hold a franchise, you have the right to trade under a name that may bring many benefits, but the condition of using the name is that you appropriately represent the company whose name you bear.

Take McDonald's as an example. Suppose I decide to launch into business by opening a McDonald's restaurant. I buy a franchise, put up the big red and yellow sign, and I am in business.

Then one day I decide to get creative, so I start thinking: *McDonald's is a wonderful Scots/Irish name, but there's nothing distinctively Scottish about the menu. So why don't I do something about it? Instead of the Big Mac, I can serve up haggis burgers. Then for breakfast I can offer oatmeal, and instead of coffee I can serve hot mugs of tea.*

It's possible I would attract some good business with my own brand of McDonald's, but when Mr. McDonald hears about this, one of the company representatives is going to visit my restaurant. He will not be impressed with my creativity or with my attempt to extend the appeal of McDonald's. Instead, he will say, "Now look here, Smith, if you carry our name, you serve our menu. And if you don't serve our menu, we're going to remove our name from you, and for misusing our name we will prosecute you to the full extent of the law."

You can't use the name McDonald's to endorse your own thing, and you can't use the name of God like that either.

The One Sin That Will Not Be Forgiven
"You shall not misuse the name of the LORD your God,
for the LORD will not hold anyone guiltless who
misuses his name."—Exodus 20:7, emphasis added

The sin of misusing God's name is so serious that God puts this offense in a category of its own. This is the only time in the Ten Commandments that God speaks about a sin for which there will be lasting guilt. "Don't expect to be forgiven for this one," God is saying. "I will not hold you guiltless."

Perhaps that surprises you. "Wait a minute," you may say. "Are you suggesting that there is a sin that is unforgivable?"

Yes.

The third commandment points directly to two New Testament Scriptures that speak about a sin for which there is no forgiveness. Significantly, both of these Scriptures relate to misusing God's name—one to blaspheming the name of God's Son, and the other to blaspheming the name of God's Spirit.

The book of Hebrews teaches that forgiveness comes through the name of Jesus and that a person who renounces Jesus loses all that He offers.

It is impossible for those who have once been enlightened, who have tasted the heavenly gift, who have shared in the Holy Spirit, who have tasted the goodness of the word of God and the powers of the coming age, if they fall away, to be brought back to repentance, because to their loss they are crucifying the Son of God all over again and subjecting him to public disgrace. (Hebrews 6:4–6)

This is a difficult passage, but it is making a simple point. The book of Hebrews was written to encourage a group of Jewish believers who were under great pressure to renounce the faith in Christ. The writer calls these believers to stay the course, and argues that if they renounce their faith in Jesus, there is no other way in which they can get right with God.

Why? Because renouncing Jesus would mean turning away from the Holy Spirit, from the gift of heaven, and from the Word of God. It would mean leaving the path on which forgiveness for the past and power for the future is found. Renouncing Jesus would mean turning back to their sins.

Jesus makes repentance possible. We can't achieve it on our own. So a man who turns away from Jesus removes himself from the *possibility* of repentance and from the forgiveness that follows.

We know from the story of Peter that Jesus is always ready to forgive and restore a person who once denied Him but then seeks to follow Him again. Peter put his trust in the risen Lord Jesus Christ and was wonderfully restored.

But the writer of Hebrews wants to remind us that restoration never happens without Jesus. Apart from Him it is impossible, and if a person refuses to believe in His name, there is no other hope.

Blasphemy Against the Holy Spirit

Jesus taught the same truth when He said, "I tell you the truth, all the sins and blasphemies of men will be forgiven them. But whoever blasphemes against the Holy Spirit will never be forgiven; he is guilty of an eternal sin" (Mark 3:28–29).

This statement has troubled many people who wonder whether at some time they may have committed this unforgivable sin of blaspheming against the Holy Spirit. Let's take a moment to understand what our Lord is saying.

Jesus had been healing the sick and casting out demons. Nobody at the time could dispute the miracles He had performed, and so His enemies suggested that He was operating by the power of the devil. "He is possessed by Beelzebub!" they said. "By the prince of demons he is driving out demons" (v. 22).

Jesus brought God's blessing into the lives of many. His enemies saw this, but they still rejected Him and pronounced His work to be demonic. This was the greatest misjudgment a person could ever make. "What you have seen is work of the Holy Spirit," Jesus told them, "And if you turn away from the work that He is doing, there is no hope for you."

It's the same message that we found in Hebrews: Forgiveness is only possible if you will embrace the One who forgives. Salvation is only possible if you come to the One who saves. Repentance that leads to lasting change can only happen through the power of the One who makes that repentance possible.

The Bible does not teach that anyone who misuses the name of God, Jesus, or the Holy Spirit will inevitably go to hell. But it does teach that unless you make the right use of God's name you will not go to heaven.

The right way of using God's name is to call upon Him in faith. Both the Old and the New Testaments make it clear that those who call upon the name of the Lord will be saved (Joel 2:32; Acts 2:21; Romans 10:13).

The prophet Joel declared, "Everyone who calls on the name of the LORD [Yahweh; that name again] will be saved" (Joel 2:32). On the day of Pentecost, Peter quoted these words and explained that calling on the name of the Lord means putting your trust in Jesus, because He is the One by whom Yahweh has made Himself known.

God offers forgiveness to every person. He offers forgiveness for every sin, including blasphemies against the name of Jesus, denials of Jesus, blasphemies against the Holy Spirit, and misuse of God's own name.

The way for you to be forgiven is to embrace the One who forgives in repentance and faith. The only sin that is unforgivable would be your continuing refusal to come and receive what God offers you in Jesus. In that case, your guilt would remain. Why would you choose such a wretched position when the invitation is open for you to call upon Him today?

Honoring the Name of Christ

God's answer to a world that blasphemes His name is a community of people who honor His name!

Isaiah the prophet was given an insight into the heart of God when he heard God's anguished cry over the abuse of His name: "All day long my name is constantly blasphemed." That's the tragedy of our world. But God has an answer: "Therefore my people will know my name" (Isaiah 52:5–6).

Those who know and love the Lord are the guardians of His reputation on the earth.

Honoring the Lord's name is our highest calling. Christ will be honored when the world sees a community of people who show awe and reverence for Him. That means growing in humility. We cannot draw attention to the greatness of God and to our own gifts or achievements at the same time.

Our calling is not to pretend that we have the answers to life's mysteries. We don't. The secret things belong to the Lord; only the revealed things belong to us. So let's not bring discredit on the gospel by claiming more than God has promised or declaring less than He has revealed. That kind of arrogance often causes other people to blaspheme the name of God.

Our calling is to share what God has given us in Christ and to invite people to the Scriptures where they can consider the claims and the evidence of Jesus.

The fact that Christians bear the name of Christ is the highest motivation for pursuing a life of integrity. The deepest impression that many people will have of the Lord will come through what they see of Him in you. That's why the apostle Peter says, "Live such good lives among the pagans that, though they accuse you of doing wrong, they may see your good deeds and glorify God on the day he visits us" (I Peter 2:12).

Throughout this world, where God's name is blasphemed every day, God is gathering communities of believers who love and worship the name of Jesus. As you grasp His love for you more deeply, you will grow in your love for Him. That will shape the way that you speak about Him, and people will begin to see that He is so much more than a name to you.

Note

1. David Wells, *God in the Wasteland* (Grand Rapids: Eerdmans, 1994), 88.

"REMEMBER THE SABBATH DAY BY KEEPING IT HOLY. SIX DAYS YOU SHALL LABOR AND DO ALL YOUR WORK, BUT THE SEVENTH DAY IS A SABBATH TO THE LORD YOUR GOD. ON IT YOU SHALL NOT DO ANY WORK."

◆EXODUS 20:8–10

Am I living

a balanced life?

four

Your Struggle
with Time

WHEN OUR BOYS WERE YOUNG we enjoyed visiting the Pizza Hut near our home. We were on a tight budget, so we would split the pizza and share the salad. The deal with the salad was that you were given a small bowl to fill, and they were pretty strict about visiting the salad bar only once.

This challenge stimulated my creativity, and I developed the art of obtaining enough salad for four people in one visit. The technique was simple: Fill the bowl with salad, add a ring of sliced cucumbers round the rim of the bowl, and then go on building higher!

The challenge of how much salad Dad could get into a small bowl became a source of family entertainment and sometimes embarrassment. The problem, of course, came in walking back from the salad bar to the table. Attempting to balance an overfilled plate, you know that you are one step from disaster.

It's always easier to fill the plate than to carry it. I've discovered that throughout my life, not just in the Pizza Hut. The overfilled plate of our lives leaves us unable to walk freely, and we often feel that we are just one step away from disaster.

The demands of working life go on increasing. More and more people feel controlled by their work, and these pressures often lead to increasingly frazzled families. A person can feel like a cog in a machine, and a family can feel like an economic convenience more than a cradle of nurturing love.

The battle against time is one of the great struggles of modern life. How should we determine priorities? What can we leave undone? How do we balance all the responsibilities of our lives? In our 24/7 culture, we desperately need to hear what God has to say about the issue of time.

The fourth commandment has often been misunderstood. Some Christians have thought that they were honoring God by making Sunday the dullest day of the week, a day marked by long lists of things that you could not do, rather than a day of delight.

I have met many believers who look back on a childhood where the day of rest was a day of misery and boredom. Their experience has left them with a deep suspicion that God's laws are restrictive rules that load you with guilt and spoil your fun. But what kind of God would do that? Certainly not the God of the Bible who always seeks our good.

So let's approach this commandment with the conviction that God's laws frame the good life that He wants us to enjoy. The fourth commandment is the longest of the ten and is divided into two parts. The first deals with the dignity of work, and the second, the blessing of rest.

The Dignity of Work

"Remember the Sabbath day by keeping it holy.
Six days you shall labor and do all your work."——Exodus 20:8–9

The fourth commandment begins by commending the dignity of work: "Six days you shall labor and do all your work." God says, "You should work for six days."

Work is a good gift from God. It began in the garden of Eden when God gave Adam the world's first job description. He was to fill the earth and subdue it; he was to work the garden of Eden and take care of it.

God gave this work to Adam before sin entered the world, and He will give new and wonderfully fulfilling work to you in His new creation. In this fallen world, we may expect some frustration, difficulty, and pain in our work; but even so, work remains a good gift from God.

The dignity of work is rooted in the nature of God. At the beginning of the Bible, God introduces Himself as a worker, who expresses Himself by creating. We are made in His image, and that means that we express ourselves by creating as well. That could mean building a car, making art or music, writing a document, or creating a home for a family to enjoy.

Your work is an expression of the image of God in you, and it's worth thinking about how your work reflects His character. Work as simple as cleaning out a closet reflects the God who creates order out of chaos. Holding a stop sign for children to cross the road creates an environment of safety that reflects the God who protects. The person who flips burgers is providing food, which is something that God does. A father or mother who nurtures a child reflects the love, patience, and perseverance of God. The CEO of a large business holds things together and moves things forward. This too is a reflection of God's work.

The Bible speaks about God both as a manual worker and as an executive worker. The psalmist describes the creation as the work of

God's "hands." The God of the Bible gets His hands dirty. When He came among us, He became a carpenter. Indeed, Jesus was known as *the* carpenter, as if there wasn't another one around who could match the quality of His work.

But God is also an executive worker. He works through His words and makes things happen by issuing commands. The heavens were made by the word of the Lord (Psalm 33:6).

So God gives dignity by His own example to the manual worker and the executive director. That's helpful because there can be a lot of tension between these two. The executive can look down his nose at the tradesman, and the tradesman can despise the pen pusher at his desk. God gives dignity to both because both reflect the pattern of God's work revealed in Scripture.

Understanding Your Work

The first step in fulfilling this command is to clearly identify the work God has given you to do. Your first instinct may be to think of work only in terms of something done for payment. But that is not a biblical view of work.

Adam was not paid for his work in the garden, and God did not create the moon and the stars because He needed the money. Those who think of work as something that they have to do in order to get money have missed the biblical vision of what work is all about. Work is more than a way of making money. It is about fulfilling the responsibility that God has given to you. Your work includes everything that God has given you to do.

One of the many problems with viewing work as something that a person does for payment is that it leads us to a completely unbiblical view of retirement. I've met retired folks who feel that since they no longer need to earn money, it follows that there is no more work for them to do.

But the Bible tells us that God has "prepared [good works] in advance for us to do" (Ephesians 2:10), and it doesn't say that they stop when you retire. I have often noticed that the people who retire most happily are those who have a clear sense of purpose for their retirement.

Your work will change with the years, and there may be circumstances where it is limited. But as long as God gives you breath, He has something useful for you to do.

Another problem with the secular view of work as something that you do for payment is that it undermines the dignity of people who are looking for work. As I write, I think of friends who would like to have paid work but find themselves between jobs. Their work is to look for work. They don't get paid for looking, but this is real work, and they need the encouragement of knowing that there is dignity in this work as they do it to the best of their ability.

It is possible to glorify God in the determination and the perseverance that you show in your search for work. If that's your situation, don't get discouraged. Don't fall into that deadly trap of becoming passive in your search. Glorify God by the way you tackle the work of looking for employment.

God calls some people to give themselves fully to work that brings no financial reward. Think of care providers who give themselves to serving people in great need, or homemakers who give themselves to caring for children and creating a home, or volunteers who serve in hospitals, schools, and churches. There is no payment for this work, but there is great dignity in it, because it reflects the character of God.

If you can see your work as an expression of the image of God, you will have an entirely different view of your work. It will bring a new dignity to the work that you do, and you will find a new joy in doing it for God's glory.

Dividing Your Work

"Six days you shall labor. . . . For in six days the LORD made
the heavens and the earth, the sea, and all that is in them."——verses 9, 11

God could have made the world in an instant, so why did He choose to make the world in six days? The answer would seem to be that God was modeling a pattern of how we should divide our work.

God has divided time into days, weeks, months, seasons, and years, and in the creation He has demonstrated the rhythms of work and rest that should mark each day and each week.

The order of God's work in creation shows the importance of structure in our work. There will be times when your work will seem like an overwhelming mountain that looks impossible to climb, and if you allow yourself to be overwhelmed, you will lose your ability to function.

The successful worker learns to divide his or her work and establish priorities. Begin by writing down what you need to do in a year; then break it down into what you will attempt in a month, then a week, and then write down what you need to do today.

Developing a plan for your work reflects the ordered pattern in which God approached His work of creation, and it's worth doing for work in the home as well as in paid employment. The less structure that you have for your work, the more you will need to develop a plan to get it done.

Nothing is more paralyzing than sitting in front of a massive task that hasn't been broken down into ordered steps. So divide your work into bite-sized chunks.

Learn to see each day as a separate opportunity for work. Tackle what needs to be done today and then rest. That's why God gave you the night. Look at six days as a unit of work and then take a day of rest. That's why God gave you the Sabbath. Plan in times of vacation. God gave that pattern through the festivals that He gave to His people spread through the year. Plan your vacations in advance so that you can savor the joy of anticipation.

Completing Your Work

"Six days you shall labor and do all your work."
——verse 9, emphasis added

We all know the phrase, "a woman's work is never done." There is some truth in that, and it is true of a man's work as well. But a woman's work for a single day can be done, as can the work of a man.

Divide your time as God did, and you will be able to enjoy completing your work. At the end of each day, God saw that His work was good. You don't find God saying, "I've made the moon and the stars, but I haven't gotten around to the fish and the animals, and I'm nowhere near starting on the man!" Instead, God enjoyed His completed work at the end of each day.

Too often, I feel burdened by what I have to do tomorrow more than I find pleasure in what God enabled me to do today. But God's pattern is that we should savor the joy of our completed work every day, every week, every season, and every year.

The Blessing of Rest

"He rested on the seventh day. Therefore the LORD *blessed the Sabbath day and made it holy."*——verse 11

Rest is the enjoyment of completed work. That's what God did on the seventh day. Having finished His work of creation, He rested because it was complete.

God calls us to follow His pattern by keeping the Sabbath day holy. The word *holy* means separate or different, not bound up with the rest. So God is calling us to make one day different from the rest of the others so that we can savor the joy of what has been completed.

Making this day different obviously depends on what you are doing on the other six days of the week. For the student it would mean making sure that you enjoy one day when you do not study.

For the manual worker it would mean enjoying one day when you are not engaged in physical labor. For the executive worker it would mean enjoying a day free from meetings and documents. For the athlete it may mean enjoying one day when you do not train. God wants us to enjoy the rhythms of rest and work in every sphere of life.

Some people have responsibilities from which it is very difficult to rest. I'm thinking especially of single parents, those who care for the elderly, or parents of special-needs children. It takes a community to make it possible for folks with unrelenting responsibilities to enjoy the blessing of the Sabbath. God's pattern for your life includes a day when you enjoy resting from the work that you normally do.

One way of doing that might be to offer help to someone whose responsibilities are very different from yours, so that they too could enjoy the blessing of the Sabbath. Helping another person to find rest by shouldering their burden for one day in the week is a wonderful way of keeping the fourth commandment.

Enjoying Your Rest

God's pattern of resting on the seventh day reminds us that we can enter into rest only when we have completed our work. We do not rest in order that we will be able to work; we work so that we will be able to rest.

Abraham Heschel has written about the Sabbath with great beauty, offering insightful Jewish wisdom on God's purpose in the fourth commandment. He describes the Sabbath as "the climax of living." It is an anticipation of the day when all our work will be complete and God's people will celebrate together in the full splendor of His immediate presence.

The Sabbath is a window in time that helps us to strengthen our grip on eternity. Every week you do your work, and then when it is done, you enter into your rest. Enlarge that snapshot of one week and you have a picture of your whole life. You pursue the work that God has given you to do, and when that work is complete, you will enter His rest, where you will enjoy the blessing of His immediate presence in the company of His people.

Discovering God's rich purpose in giving us the gift of the Sabbath will help you discern how best to spend your day of rest. You will want to enjoy God's presence in worship, and you will want the day to be filled with pleasure as you savor the joy of completing your work. Knowing that God intends the day of rest to be the climax of living will help you to view it with eager anticipation.

Sharing Your Rest
"The seventh day is a Sabbath to the LORD your God.
On it you shall not do any work, neither you, nor your son or daughter,
nor your manservant or maidservant, nor your animals,
nor the alien within your gates."—verse 10

God calls us to share the blessing of rest with everyone in our sphere of influence: your family, the folk who work for you, the alien, and even the animals.

Rest often seems to be the privilege of those who can afford it. The company executive may be able to spend extended time at his country club while the minimum-wage immigrant worker finds that he has to work without a break in order to scratch a living. That's how it is in the world, but God calls His people to model a different set of values, making sure that everyone within their sphere of influence is able to enjoy the day of rest.

Work was unrelenting when God's people were slaves in Egypt. There was no Sabbath there. But God released them from that pattern of life and called them to create a different kind of community that would reflect His glory.

When the nations looked at God's people, they would see that even the animals were given a day of rest. Imagine the impact of this testimony to the surrounding nations who did not know Yahweh. By the pattern of their lives, God's people were saying, "God has given us work to do, but He has made us for eternity, so every week we rest from our work to taste what He has prepared for us."

I'm convinced that we desperately need to rediscover and practice the principle of the fourth commandment. In the relentlessness of our modern lives, a community of people who have learned how to rest would attract a lot of attention to Jesus.

Sabbaths and Sundays

Jesus rose from the dead on the first day of the week, and Christians have worshiped on the first day ever since. Believers hold different opinions about whether Sunday should be regarded as a new Sabbath. Some say that Sunday is the Christian Sabbath, while others say that the day of rest and the day of worship are two different things.

Sunday would normally have been a working day for the first Christians. They would meet for worship early in the morning before going to work, or late at night after a full working day. That may be why Eutychus fell asleep and then fell out of the window while Paul was preaching an especially long sermon!

I find great significance in the decision of the first believers to worship on the first day of the week. The Old Testament law about the seventh day calls us to finish our work in order that we may enter our rest. That principle holds true for us with regard to our work. We cannot rest until our work is done. But the New Testament speaks of another kind of rest that we enter on an entirely different basis.

As we have begun to consider everything that God has called us to do in the Ten Commandments, it has already become clear that we haven't finished this work. We struggle to embrace God unconditionally, to worship Him as He is, and to use His name in a way that brings Him honor.

With the help of God's Spirit we may have begun the work of fulfilling God's commands, but we are very far from finishing that work. Indeed, as we understand these commands more deeply, it will become increasingly obvious that we will never finish this work.

That leads to a fundamental question: If I cannot finish the work of keeping God's commandments, how can I hope to enter into God's rest? How can you enter God's rest if you have not completed all that He called you to do?

It would be possible only if someone else completed the work for you, and that is precisely what Jesus Christ has done. When He died on the cross, He took all our unfinished business on Himself. He bore all of our sins and our falling short of God's Law in His own body. Then He cried out with a loud voice, "It is finished!"

My work is far from finished, but Christ's work is complete. That is why Jesus is able to say, "Come to me . . . and I will give you rest" (Matthew 11:28). You have not finished what God has called you to do, but He has, and He can give you rest for your soul. That is something that you can never achieve, even by a lifetime of effort to please God.

I love the fact that Christians worship on the first day of the week. It reminds me that I begin my work from a position of enjoying rest with God through the finished work of Christ.

God has work for me to do, but I'm not doing it to earn my salvation. The purpose of my work is not to prove myself to God or to anyone else. Christ's finished work sets me free to offer my work as a loving expression of gratitude and worship, flowing out of the rest that I find in Him.

"HONOR YOUR FATHER AND
YOUR MOTHER, SO THAT
YOU MAY LIVE LONG IN
THE LAND THE LORD YOUR
GOD IS GIVING YOU."

◆EXODUS 20:12

Do I love the people

God has placed around me?

five

Your Struggle
with Authority

IT'S EASY TO TALK about loving other people in general terms.
The problem comes with the difficult personalities of the people God
puts next to you. That might include your mother, father, brother, sister, son, or daughter, along with your demanding teacher, noisy neighbor, struggling pastor, difficult boss, and your unscrupulous business
competitor.

It would be relatively easy to love your neighbor if you could
choose who that neighbor would be, but God doesn't give you that
luxury. God chooses the people who come into your life. They will include some folk who are easy to love and others who are difficult.

In the first four commandments, God explains what it would mean
for you to love Him with all your heart, mind, soul, and strength. Love
begins in your relationship with God: knowing that He has loved you,

and learning to love Him in response. But it does not end there. God wants you to love other people as much as you love yourself. That's the focus of this fifth commandment and the others that follow. That love for others begins with displaying love for those who raise us, our parents.

Your First Struggle with Authority

The first people God puts in your life are your father and your mother. Parents are the first authority figures in our lives, and this command opens up the whole dimension of how we relate to the people God places in authority over us.

Your first experience of a person with authority will shape your reaction to other authorities. If, in your early experience, you saw parental authority used well, you will most likely have an instinctive respect for people who are given authority in other areas of life. But if you experienced the abuse of authority, you may find that you are instinctively suspicious of authority, and you want to establish your independence from it.

Respect for authority is learned in the home. That's why the strength and healthy functioning of family life is so important to the good of the nation. If respect for authority breaks down in the home, it will soon crumble in the school, the workplace, the community, and the nation.

A culture will not survive long when respect for authority breaks down in the home. That's why God says, "Honor your father and mother, so that you may live long in the land."

Your parents are unique, and your experiences with them are too. While many people share similar family experiences, nobody has exactly the same perspective as you. Some children were privileged to enjoy the blessing of being raised in a stable and loving home. Others were not.

If your parents brought disappointment and pain into your life, you may find that your defenses go up as you read this commandment. Your first instinct may be to fear that God's Word will hurt you. Your parents hurt you, and they were the first authority figures in your life. You conclude that God is like them and that He will do the same.

One of the greatest struggles for those who have suffered from poor parenting is to avoid projecting the failures of inadequate parents onto God and assuming that God has the same failings as those who let you down. The projections of your imagination will always mislead you. That's why it is so important to discover what God is like from the Bible. Yahweh is good, and He wants to do you good. Don't let the warped authority of your parents blind you to the loving authority of God.

The fifth commandment would be easy if it said, "Honor your father and mother as long as they are honorable," but God doesn't say that. God does not allow us the luxury of choosing whom we should honor. He puts certain people in our lives. Some of them are easy to honor; with others, it is extremely difficult.

The fifth commandment confronts us with some difficult questions that we have to face honestly: How should a Christian student respond to a difficult teacher? How should an employee deal with a difficult boss? How should Christians relate to leaders in the church or in the nation with whom they may passionately disagree? What is your responsibility when a person in authority behaves dishonorably? What would it mean to honor them?

The Meaning of "Honor"

The word "honor" in the fifth commandment literally means "give weight to" or "regard as heavy." So literally translated, the commandment says, "Regard your father and your mother as heavy." "Give weight to your father and your mother." If one of your parents is a few pounds overweight, you will find this easy to remember!

When your father or mother says something, don't take it lightly. Listen to your parents' advice. Don't brush it off; take it seriously. Give weight to what they say, to what they think, and to what they desire. What this looks like will change through the course of life, but the principle remains the same.

For young children, honoring your father and mother simply means doing what they ask. "Children, obey your parents in the Lord, for this is right" (Ephesians 6:1). Jesus Himself is our example. The Bible tells us that in His childhood, He was obedient to His parents (Luke 2:51).

I often tell children who love the Lord that the best way they can honor Him is to do what their mom or dad tells them, and to do it cheerfully. Children who learn to show love to their parents in their early years will develop their capacity to love others as they grow into maturity.

Moving through adolescence, honoring your father and mother will mean making a full contribution to family life. Don't regard your home as a bed-and-breakfast, or your parents as a cash point and laundry service. You are a member of a family, and God wants you to make the life of that family richer through your influence. Beyond doing what your parents say, help around the house and contribute to family life.

As you launch into adult life, the relationship with your parents changes again. You are no longer under the obligation of obedience, but God still calls you to give them honor. The fifth commandment does not say "Honor your father and your mother while you are young." There are no term limits on the love God calls you to show to the people He has placed next to you in life.

As an adult son or daughter, learn the joy that comes by visiting parents and talking with them often. You honor them with your presence and sharing your life with them, so make an effort to visit them— or invite them on a vacation with you. Show by your actions that you respect their opinions and feelings and care about their welfare.

It's important to understand the way that honoring your father and mother changes as you move into adult life, and especially if you choose to be married.

When God established marriage, He specifically said that a man should leave his father and mother and be united to his wife (Genesis 2:24). The man's first loyalty changes, as does the primary loyalty of his wife. The new couple is not to live under the control of either set of parents. They are not in charge—not even by remote control! A man or woman who is not able to establish his or her independence from their parents is not ready for marriage.

I often encourage those who are considering marriage or making other major life decisions to weigh the opinions of their parents. Your mother and father are not always right, but they do know you, and they have seen more of life than you have.

Listen to what they have to say in the big decisions of life. Give weight to it. Think about it deeply. Say to yourself with a sense of gravity, "This is the opinion of *my mother and my father.*"

When Your Parents Are Wrong

Having said that, remember that honoring your parents in adult life does not mean going along with everything that they say. Your parents can be wrong.

Jesus faced this experience early in His ministry, when His mother and His brothers tried to hold Him back from His God-given mission (Mark 3:21, 31). But Jesus did not allow them to stop Him from doing the will of God. His handling of this issue is a wonderful model for those who face this difficult conflict of loyalties.

The path of wisdom in adult life is neither to follow your parents' advice with slavish obedience nor to brush it off as of little value. Honor your parents by giving weight to what they say. Then decide the right course of action, remembering that your loyalty is first to God, and second, if married, to your husband or wife. Give weight to the words of each in the proportion that is due. A wise parent will see this and support it.

Following childhood, adolescence, and your young adult years comes the final stage of a relationship with your parents, when your father and mother reach old age. Honoring your parents in their later years means giving weight to their needs.

Once again, Jesus is our example. During the hours of His excruciating agony on the cross, our Lord showed the depth of His love for His mother when He commissioned John to care for her. Looking down from the cross, Jesus saw His mother, Mary, standing next to John. "Dear woman," He said, "here is your son." Then to John He said, "Here is your mother." The Bible records that from that time John took Mary, the mother of Jesus, into his home (John 19:26–27).

The priority that Jesus gave to the future care of His mother, even while He was engaged in the work of saving the world, shows the value of caring for a father or mother in the heart of God. Even in His suffering, Christ was obeying and fulfilling the fifth commandment as He gave weight to the needs of His mother.

It's easy for us to become so busy with important things that we forget or neglect the honor that God has called us to give to our parents. Visiting or phoning parents can be an important part of honoring them, as well as doing what we can to make sure that they are well cared for. The apostle Paul shows the importance of these things when he says, "If anyone does not provide for his relatives, and especially for his immediate family, he has denied the faith and is worse than an unbeliever" (I Timothy 5:8).

There is no formula for how this is to be done, but the principle is clear: Those who follow Christ are to give weight to the needs and interests of their parents.

Parenting Worthy of Honor

Since God's will for children is that they honor their parents, it follows that God's calling for parents is to create an environment that helps their children fulfill this command. The apostle Paul makes it clear that the proper use of authority is included within the scope of the fifth commandment. Quoting the command for children to honor their father and mother (Ephesians 6:2–3), he shows what this means for parents: "Fathers, do not exasperate your children; instead, bring them up in the training and instruction of the Lord" (verse 4).

If you're a parent, you have an awesome responsibility. God gives the gift of children, and they are a sacred trust from His hand. As the first authority figure in the life of your child, you will play a significant role in shaping their knowledge and understanding of God.

The Bible tells us that God is our Father and that all fatherhood comes from Him (Ephesians 3:14–15). Becoming a father or a mother means representing God in the life of your child.

Think of all the ways in which you stand in the place of God for your child. You are the child's guardian, provider, shepherd, intercessor, teacher, and example. What your child experiences from you will shape that child's impressions of God. Your calling is to give them a good reflection of the image of God. That is the highest calling of parenthood.

It's also the greatest challenge. Representing God well before your children means, for example, that you need to be responsive to the requests of your children, because you want them to know that this is what God is like. But you dare not give them everything that they want because that would be a misrepresentation of God.

You need to show them that you will never stop loving them, because that is what God is like. But you also need them to understand that when they choose a wrong path, it always brings painful consequences. If you don't teach them this in their early years, you misrepresent God.

As parents, we need our children to see that we are on their side, that we are for them, that we will stick with them through times of trouble and will always seek their good, because that is what God is like. We also need them to know that when they choose a wrong path, our aim is to bring them back, not to confirm them in their folly, because otherwise we misrepresent God.

The highest purpose of all parenting is to show what God is like, and that is why becoming a parent is a great incentive for knowing Christ. How can you do this job if you do not walk with Him?

Of all the materials that are available on parenting today, there is no greater resource than the Word of God. Learning who God is will give you the ultimate template for parenting.

How to Use Your Authority

If God has given you authority in the home, in His church, or in your work, you need to know how to use that authority effectively. Good parents and effective leaders exercise their authority within three boundaries, which you can picture as the sides of a triangle. They are wisdom, sufficiency, and love. Abuse begins when authority is used outside these lines.

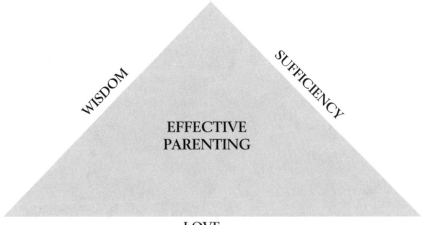

Authority and Wisdom

King Solomon recorded some wisdom for parents in the book of Proverbs. "Train a child in the way he should go," he said, "and when he is old he will not turn from it" (Proverbs 22:6).

Notice that Solomon speaks about one child rather than children in general. While we teach the same moral principles to all of our children, the wise parent will remember that no two children are the same. Raising children would be much easier if there were a single formula for the way that they should go. But Solomon has no such formula. His call is to discern the way that an individual child should go and to train him or her in that direction.

Recently I enjoyed watching a rodeo on television. Texas cowboys perched precariously on the backs of bulls were desperately trying to hold on for ten seconds. Apparently, most of them had broken just about every bone in their bodies at some time in their careers.

What fascinated me was the way that these cowboys knew each of the bulls by name, and seemed to have some awareness of how each one might turn. Knowing the bull was the key to sustaining the ride. That might be a good picture for the task of parenting! No two children are ever the same, so guide each one with wisdom.

Years ago, a wise friend encouraged me to distinguish between the cosmetic and the corrupting. I've found that to be a helpful distinction. Don't make a big deal over a passing phase that has little consequence, but be sure you don't turn a blind eye to that which will corrupt.

God parents all of His children with consummate wisdom and skill. He knows exactly how to handle each child in every situation. On one occasion, God spoke of His child Israel behaving like a wild donkey (Hosea 8:9). But on another occasion, He spoke of the same child as a bruised reed and said that He would not break the bruised reed or snuff the smoking wick (Isaiah 42:3).

Wisdom can tell when your child is being a wild donkey and when he or she is like a bruised reed. Discern the difference and then you will know how to use your strength.

Authority and Sufficiency

Sufficiency is the second boundary for the exercise of your authority. When a father or mother uses a child to meet his or her unfulfilled needs, authority can quickly slide into abuse.

Parents who have not fulfilled their own hopes and dreams can easily slide into living these out through their children. The father drives his son to achieve what he hoped to become. The mother drives the daughter to be the person she wanted to become. These impulses are sometimes hidden deep within our hearts, but they can often be destructive in family life.

A father or mother who has not felt loved may also try to find what they lack in their child, but that will prevent Dad or Mom from parenting effectively. Parents sometimes have to make unpopular decisions, and if you have become emotionally dependent on your child, you won't be able to do that.

A wise father once said to his son, "If I ever have to choose between being your father and your friend, I will always choose the role of your father. You have many friends, but you have only one father."

Parents who become emotionally dependent on their children will also be in difficulties when the time comes for these children to establish their independence.

Using your children to fulfill your unmet needs will bring damage both to them and to you. The same will be true in your work, your ministry, your marriage, or anything else that you try to put into the space that only God can fill. The healthy parent is the one who finds his or her sufficiency in God and therefore is free to serve those God has placed in his or her care.

Authority and Love

The third boundary for exercising authority is love. Authority without love is always destructive. This is especially important for

Christian parents. Sometimes, we can long so deeply for our children to follow Christ that we run the risk of manipulation.

A compliant child will often be willing to say a prayer of commitment to Jesus because they want to please you, and they know that this is what you want them to do.

If that happens, you may find yourself telling a child that he or she has been saved and that the Holy Spirit lives within them when they really haven't experienced any inner transformation, with the result that in later life they conclude that Christian faith has no substance and is only an empty shell.

Parents, pastors, and Sunday school teachers need to be especially careful about putting pressure on children to profess faith or to be baptized. Love woos but never forces, and a wise parent will discern the difference.

When Dr. Lloyd-Jones's daughter Elizabeth was in her early teens, a family friend asked the preacher, "Don't you think that you should have a talk with her?" by which he meant that Dr. Lloyd-Jones should initiate a direct attempt to lead his daughter to a commitment of faith in Christ. The doctor replied simply, "She will come when she is ready."

In his book on the Christian family, Lloyd-Jones described a meeting in which pressure is placed on children to make a decision for Christ. "That should never be done," he wrote. "You are violating the personality of the child. In addition, of course, you are displaying a profound ignorance of the way of salvation. You can make a little child decide anything. You have the power and the ability to do so; but it is wrong, it is unchristian, it is unspiritual."

Later, he continued, "We must never be too direct in this matter especially with a child, never be too emotional. If your child feels uncomfortable as you are talking to him about spiritual matters, or if you are talking to someone else's child and he feels uncomfortable, your method is obviously wrong. . . . You are bringing pressure to bear. That is not the way to do this work."[1]

Maybe you are wondering where you can find the wisdom, sufficiency, and love that you need for parenting your children. The answer is that you will find all these things in God Himself. He is our wisdom, and He is completely self-sufficient, the great "I AM." He is not dependent on anybody, and is able to pour His love into your life, so that your parenting may give a true reflection of Him.

Honoring Unworthy Parents

Some parents are not worthy of honor, and knowing how to relate to unworthy parents can be one of the greatest struggles of life.

The Bible has plenty of examples. Saul was both an ineffective king and an abusive father. His son Jonathan had to endure Saul's wild mood swings, his fits of rage, and his sometimes irrational behavior. On one occasion, Saul threw a spear at Jonathan, intending "to kill him" (1 Samuel 20:33). What kind of father throws a spear at his son?

God knows about the hidden abuse that goes on in too many families. Bad parenting brings great pain and can leave deep wounds that only God is able to heal. God knows the truth, and He does not ask you to pretend that bad parents were good or that a neglectful parent is honorable.

The obvious question is how can you honor a parent or, indeed, anybody else in a position of authority who has been and may still be dishonorable?

You may find it helpful to think about the unworthy parent as one who did not have the wisdom, sufficiency, or love to do their job well. What they did not receive, they were not able to give. Seeing their need may help you to have compassion and may keep you from bitterness.

If your parents are still in that position, you may feel alienated from them. But even if the relationship has broken down, you can still ask God to give you compassion for them. Pray that God will give them what they lack. That's the Spirit of Jesus: He does not treat us as our sins deserve. He wants us to know that the door to reconciliation is always open on His side, and He reaches out to draw us in that direction.

If you have suffered through abused authority, you may have feared the authority of God, and therefore kept at a distance from Him. But the healing of many wounds will begin as you look away from the failings of your parents and up into the face of God. He will make it possible for you to break free from the cycle of unworthy parenting that otherwise might be passed on from one generation to another. Discovering His wisdom, sufficiency, and love through Jesus Christ can bring new hope for your life and for your family.

Note

1. Martyn Lloyd-Jones, *Life in the Spirit in Marriage, Home and Work* (Edinburgh, Scotland: Banner of Truth, 1973), 298.

"YOU SHALL NOT MURDER."

◆EXODUS 20:13

Am I harboring anger,

hatred, or bitterness?

six

Your Struggle
for Peace

IF YOU CAME INTO MY OFFICE, one of the first things you would see is a portrait of my wife. The picture was taken in a studio some years ago, and I treasure it because it captures her beauty.

If this image was left in the basement of my house for a hundred years and then was found by some future owner, he might dust off the cobwebs and say, "Oh, I wonder who she was?" and then toss the picture in the trash. But I could never trash this picture, because it bears the image of someone I love.

The reason human life is so valuable is that it bears the image of God. A lab report might tell us that a human being is made up largely of water along with some other chemicals that are of little value, but the Bible tells us that men and women are made in the likeness of God (Genesis 1:26–27).

Human life is created in God's image, and that makes it sacred. The offense in taking a human life is that it involves destroying the image of God. Yet we struggle to respect human life and to live at peace with each other. There are many ways of destroying another person's life besides homicide, and the sixth commandment comes much closer to home than you might think. In fact, it describes one of the ten greatest struggles of your life: the struggle for peace with your fellow man.

The Uniqueness of Human Life

The image of God makes human life different from every other form of life on the planet. God has given life to trees, fish, plants, and animals, but none of them bears His likeness.

God gave the plants and animals to men and women for food. "Everything that lives and moves will be food for you," God said to Noah. "Just as I gave you the green plants, I now give you everything" (Genesis 9:3). He has given us liberty to fish the seas, to farm the animals, and to harvest the fields and the forests. But human life is in a different category, and about this God says, "Whoever sheds the blood of man, by man shall his blood be shed; for in the image of God has God made man" (Genesis 9:6).

In these words, God makes it clear that a vast chasm exists between the lives of fish, plants, and animals, and the life of a man or a woman who is made in His image.

Many people today have lost sight of this chasm. Losing touch with the Creator, they have come to believe that they are simply developed animals. This has led to a great confusion, causing many to regard animals as if they were humans and humans as if they were animals.

That confusion lies at the root of the growing debate on euthanasia. The logic is simple: "I love my dog and I don't want to see it suffer. So, when my dog gets old and no longer is able to enjoy a good quality of life, I will take it to the vet and have it put down. If I can do this for the dog that I love, why should I not do the same for my grandmother?"

A society that cannot tell the difference between a dog and a grandmother has lost touch with the Bible's teaching about the unique value of human life. This is an area in which all of us who profess to believe in and worship Yahweh need to check our thinking against the teaching of His Word. There is a vast chasm that separates human life from every other form of life, and what God has separated, no one should join together.

War and Capital Punishment

When discussions about the sixth commandment get going, two controversial issues usually come up. One is the issue of war, and the other is capital punishment.

Christians have held different positions on both of these issues over many years, and there is room for legitimate debate here between people who are serious about applying the teaching of the Bible in our world today.

But these matters cannot be settled by an appeal to the sixth commandment. The same God who gave this command also gave His people the laws that call for capital punishment. And at times He led His people into battle against their enemies.

There are some situations in which, if a life or lives are taken, many other lives may be saved. David took the life of Goliath and liberated a whole generation of his people from a threat that had terrorized their nation.

But the New Testament makes it very clear that the authority for taking action of this sort is not given to individuals, but to governments, and they are given the responsibility of doing this for the protection of the people they govern. It's an awesome responsibility, and we should pray often for those who are entrusted with this task.

Murder—*Taking the Life of Your Neighbor*

The first application of the sixth commandment is that God forbids acts of murder. This would involve taking the life of your neighbor whom God calls you to love.

Somewhere in your life you may come to a situation where murder would not seem beyond you. An injury can be so great and the desire for vengeance so strong that a person feels he has the right to exercise his own justice by taking another life. But God reserves the right to bring justice for Himself. " 'It is mine to avenge; I will repay,' says the Lord" (Romans 12:19).

When Jesus was arrested, Peter drew his sword and swung it at the high priest's servant. It would have been a two-handed sword, and there is no doubt in my mind that Peter's aim was to strike this man at the center of his skull and split him in two, right down the middle. But he missed by a few inches, and all he managed to do was cut off the servant's ear. Jesus would have none of this. "Put away your sword," He said to Peter.

Then Jesus reached out and healed the man who had been struck by His disciple's sword. Christ was healing the wound that had been caused by the sin of His friend (see John 18:10–11).

Abortion—*Taking the Life of an Unborn Neighbor*

The sixth commandment speaks to the issue of abortion, which is taking the life of an unborn child.

Abortion is wrong because the unborn child is created in the image of God. A child in the womb is your unborn neighbor, and God calls you to love your unborn neighbor as much as you love yourself.

God has an active relationship with the developing life of a child in the womb. Perhaps the most beautiful expression of this is in Psalm 139, where David described God's perfect knowledge of every person.

"Where can I go from your Spirit? Where can I flee from your presence?" David asks, and then he goes through some examples of places where you might think a person could be hidden from God. "If I go up to the heavens, you are there; if I make my bed in the depths, you are there." He concludes that if he flees to the uttermost parts of the earth, "you are there" (see verses 7–10).

God's presence is everywhere, and that causes David to worship. God knows all about him, and God's presence is always with him, by day and night, in life and in death, wherever he walks on the face of the earth or even beyond.

But then David raises one more fascinating question: "What about before I was born? Did I register on God's radar screen then?" Here's the answer: "My frame was not hidden from you when I was made in the secret place. . . . Your eyes saw my unformed body. All the days ordained for me were written in your book" (verses 15–16).

God's hand is on the life of the unborn child, and that is why the unborn child should be of great value to us. This is not a potential life, but it is *a life,* with all kinds of potential.

God's care for a human life from the moment of conception is a wonderful comfort for parents who have gone through the pain of a miscarriage, and may have done so many times. The little life that was lost to you is known to God and is safe in His hands.

Euthanasia—*Taking the Life of an Elderly or Infirm Neighbor*

Euthanasia involves making a decision that a person's life is no longer worth living and that some action should be taken to end it.

There is a great difference between ending life and ending treatment. You may find yourself in a situation in which it becomes obvious that a life is ending, and the body of someone you love is being sustained by a treatment that holds no hope of recovery. Ending treatment may be a way of turning that person's life over to God.

There is a huge difference between sustaining a life that has been taken by God and taking a life that is being sustained by God.

Discerning that line can be horrendously difficult. Knowing that there is a line is crucial. Where God is sustaining a life, nobody is in a position to say that life is not worth living.

Suicide—*Taking Your Own Life*

Another application of the sixth commandment is to suicide, taking your own life, which has been made in the image of God.

At some point, you may come to a place where you feel that your life is no longer worth living. Only God knows how many people walk through this experience, but I suspect that most people may encounter a time where they feel at least for a moment, and often for much longer, that there would be no loss to the world if they were gone.

If that's where you are as you read, listen up! It's not true. God has given you life. God wants you here. This life is not yours to take. You are a steward of the life that God has given to you. You are the trustee of this life, and God is the owner.

God will stand with you in your darkness. It will take an act of faith to believe that, but you can glorify Him by holding on in your darkness. The life that He is giving to you is of irreplaceable value, and the fact that it is painful does not diminish your importance to God.

Therefore, cherish the life that He is giving to you. Even if you cannot see its value now, one day you will, and you do not want to stand in the presence of God to discover what might have been.

Christopher Reeve, the tall, athletic actor best known for his portrayal of the mighty Superman in four movies, suffered a fall from a horse and became a quadriplegic years ago. The muscular actor who had been an expert sailor, scuba diver, skier, and horseman was paralyzed from the neck down and put on a ventilator. During an interview on CNN's *Larry King Live,* Reeve explained that he contemplated suicide after his terrible accident. I was moved as he revealed that he had discussed the idea with his wife, Dana, who said, "Let's give it two years."

Larry King asked Dana, who was seated next to her husband, what she would have done if Christopher had still wanted to end his life when the two years were over. She laughed. "I was just negotiating," she said.

Her strategy in handling the crisis was wonderfully wise. She knew that when a person is in great pain, their mind is often not clear. It's important to remember that at times when you may feel your life is not worth living.

At this moment you desperately need to hear the Word of God: God says "You shall not murder." You are not to take your neighbor's life, and you are not to take your own. Hold on to God. He will hold on to you and bring you through to hope and a future (see Jeremiah 29:11).

Stations on the Line of Conflict

Now let's suppose that you go through your entire life without committing murder, having an abortion, practicing euthanasia, or committing suicide. Would that mean that you had kept the sixth commandment? Answer: No.

Jesus made it clear that the scope of this commandment goes far beyond acts of murder to the thoughts and desires of our hearts. Picture a train moving along a track on which there are many stations. Murder is the station at the far end of a line called conflict. Many of us will never go near that station, but all of us have traveled somewhere on this track. Let's visit three of the stations on the line.

Station I: Verbal Abuse

Jesus taught that abusive speech is a direct violation of the sixth commandment. He explained its significance in these words:

"You have heard that it was said to the people long ago, 'Do not murder, and anyone who murders will be subject to judgment.' But I tell you that anyone who is angry with his brother will be subject to judgment. Again, anyone who says to his brother, 'Raca,' is answerable to the Sanhedrin. But anyone who says, 'You fool!' will be in danger of the fire of hell." (Matthew 5:21–22)

Jesus was describing a situation where someone becomes angry with another person and begins to speak abusively. The word "Raca" was a term of contempt. Roughly translated, it means, "You're useless." We might call this rudeness, but Jesus makes it clear that rude, insulting, abusive, or demeaning language is a violation of the sixth commandment.

Abusive speech is an offense for which a person is accountable to God and, according to Jesus, the problem it created was not just that a person might be reported to the Sanhedrin but that their verbal violation of the sixth commandment would put them in danger of the fires of hell.

That would have gotten the attention of the crowd! If angry words that insult or diminish another person are a violation of the sixth commandment, then all of us are guilty.

The Ten Commandments are an explanation of the meaning of love, and love is not rude (1 Corinthians 13:5). If I speak about another person with contempt, I am not loving my neighbor as myself, and I am breaking the sixth commandment.

Once again, we're discovering that the Ten Commandments address the great struggles of our lives, and one of them is this whole area of conflict. We aim to live a life of love, but some people are downright difficult. They do unreasonable things that make us angry, and sometimes, when we are provoked, we give them a piece of our mind. But if we speak or act in a way that is threatening, insulting, abusive, or belittling, we are breaking the sixth commandment.

The Heidelberg Catechism, to which we referred earlier, sets this out clearly:

Q. What is God's will for you in the sixth commandment?

A. I am not to belittle, insult, hate or kill my neighbor——not by my thoughts, my words, my look or my gesture.[1]

We sometimes use the phrase, "if looks could kill," and the Catechism rightly reminds us that there are ways of looking at another person that break the sixth commandment.

The command not to murder, which many Christians assume they have kept, turns out, when properly understood, to be the commandment that we have all most clearly broken! And since Jesus makes it quite clear that breaking this command or any other puts a person in danger of the fires of hell, it may be that the commandment you were most confident of having kept will be the one that shows you how much you need the forgiveness that God offers to you through Jesus Christ.

Station 2: Hatred

The apostle John tells us that hatred is a violation of the sixth commandment. "Anyone who hates his brother is a murderer, and you know that no murderer has eternal life in him" (1 John 3:15).

One writer has pointed out that racial hatred is easily the world leader in violating the sixth commandment. More murders in our world have been inspired by racial hatred than any other single cause.[2]

Hatred leads to threats, intimidation, bullying, and violence, and God calls us to turn away from all these things in the sixth commandment. There is no place for hatred toward another person in the life of a follower of Jesus.

But Jesus calls us to go further. He crossed the racial barriers that divided Jews from Samaritans. He taught us by His words and His example to love our enemies and to do good to those who mean us harm. Christ demonstrated the power of loving our enemies in His own life and in His death. Paul reminds us that it was while *we* were still His ene-mies that Christ died for us (Romans 5:8, 10).

Following Christ today will mean showing love and kindness to those who are most despised in our community, even if they have little sympathy with or interest in the cause of Christ. It will mean do-ing what we can to protect them from harm.

Jesus embraced tax collectors and prostitutes, the most despised and hated people in the community at that time. He demonstrated the power of love, and many lives were changed as a result.

Station 3: Recklessness

God calls you to love your neighbor as yourself, and that means that He wants you to take good care of your own life. The Heidelberg Catechism includes this as part of our responsibility under the sixth commandment:

Q. What is God's will for you in the sixth commandment?
A. I am not to harm or recklessly endanger myself.[3]

You are a steward of the life that God has given you. It is of unique and irreplaceable value, so handle your own life with care.

You can break the sixth commandment by neglecting a proper pat-tern of sleep, by addiction to work, by an improper use of food, drink, or drugs, or by a lack of proper exercise.

It would be easy to feel complacent about the sixth commandment because you have never killed anybody else, while through your choices of lifestyle you are slowly killing yourself!

A culture that values life begins with a community of people who see the value of their own lives as a precious gift from God and then place the same value on every other life.

Fulfilling the Sixth Commandment

God's commandments are like warning signs on the road, telling us what to avoid. But they are also direction signs, showing us what to pursue. The sixth commandment points us in two very obvious directions: first, that we embrace life, and second, that we pursue peace.

Your life is a precious gift from God, and keeping the sixth commandment means embracing to the full the life God gives you. Ask God to give you a vision of what your life can be. Seize every opportunity to develop yourself. Look for ways in which you can be a good steward of all the gifts God has given to you. Invest your life wisely. Make the big choices of your life carefully. Turn away from the attitude that shrugs and says, "Who cares?" God cares and so should you.

Then look for ways in which you can enrich the lives of others. Seek to bring God's blessing wherever you can. Live the life God has given you to the full for His glory. There is no greater way to embrace life than to follow Jesus. He said, "I have come that they may have life, and have it to the full" (John 10:10).

When Christ explained the meaning of the sixth commandment, He applied it by saying that we should settle our disputes as quickly as possible (Matthew 5:25). This theme runs throughout the New Testament. Paul urges us, "If it is possible, as far as it depends on you, live at peace with everyone" (Romans 12:18). Peter takes up the same theme: "Whoever would love life and see good days . . . must seek peace and pursue it" (I Peter 3:10–11).

The principle is clear: If there is a way to settle a dispute with integrity, take it. That's what God wants you to do.

Jesus is the Prince of Peace. He is able to bring peace into the deepest wounds of your life, and He calls you to pursue peace with others.

Lifting the Line of Conflict

Karen and I often return to my family home in the Highlands of Scotland where we enjoy walking on a beautiful path that follows the route of an old railway track. The track was removed about fifty years ago, and people now walk through the cutting and enjoy the beauty of the surrounding view.

Those pulled rail tracks remind me of the future path of peace. The line of conflict, with its sad stations, runs all the way from abusive speech to murder. It runs through our lives and has carried heavy traffic throughout the history of the world. But one day the line of conflict will be replaced by the path of peace.

When Christ comes in His glory, He will lift the line of conflict. Nation will speak peace to nation. The implements of war will be obsolete. Under the reign of Christ you will experience the joy of true community. You will be at peace with yourself and with your neighbor.

Then, in a new heaven and earth, the whole creation will be released from its groaning under the curse. There will be no more death or mourning or crying or pain. The whole line of conflict will be gone forever, and God will make everything new.

Notes

1. Heidelberg Catechism (Grand Rapids: CRC, 1975), Question 105.

2. David Searle, *And Then There Were Nine* (Fearn, Scotland: Christian Focus, 2000), 101.

3. Heidelberg Catechism (Grand Rapids: CRC, 1975), Question 105.

Am I in control

of my sexuality?

seven

Your Struggle
for Purity

THE BEST MESSAGE I EVER HEARD on the seventh commandment was given to a class of young, elementary-age children in
our church. I had decided to see the good work that was going on in
our children's ministry and arrived in the class as the Sunday school
teacher was launching into a story that has stayed in my memory ever
since.

One day, Sam's mother asked him what he would like to do for his
birthday, which was going to be on the next Friday. "Well," said Sam,
"I'd like to have a party and a sleepover and then go fishing with Dad
in the morning."

When his mom asked who he wanted to come for the sleepover,
Sam knew right away. "I want Johnny to come," he said. "He's my best
friend, and I want it to be just the two of us."

So the next day Sam invited Johnny to the party. "It's my birthday on Friday," said Sam, "and I'd like you to come and stay for a sleepover, and then in the morning, we'll go fishing with my dad. It will just be the two of us. It will be awesome."

Johnny was really excited about the party plans, especially going to Sam's house for a sleepover.

"That will be great," he said.

"You will definitely come, right?" said Sam. "You're my best friend, and you are the only one I've invited."

"Of course I'll come," said Johnny, "I'll be there on Friday, I promise."

A few days before the party, Luke, another boy in the same class at school, spoke to Johnny.

"Hey, Johnny," he said. "I'm having a party and I'd really like you to come. It's going to be at Chuck E. Cheese's; everyone's going to be there, and then we're all coming back to my place for a sleepover in tents!"

Johnny loved Chuck E. Cheese's, and when he asked who else was invited, he found that his other friends were all going to Luke's party.

"That will be great," he said. "When is the party?"

"It's on Friday," said Luke.

Johnny didn't know what to do. He had promised to go to Sam's party, but now he felt like he wanted to go to Luke's as well.

Later that day, Johnny saw Sam on the playground.

"Look, Sam," he said, "I'm not sure if I can come to your party."

"Why not?" said Sam.

"Luke asked me to go to his party and I really want to go there."

Sam didn't say anything, but later when he arrived home, he cried and cried. In fact, he couldn't stop crying. Sam's mother found him sobbing and wanted to know what was wrong.

"Johnny told me he was coming to my party," said Sam. "He promised. But now he doesn't want to come."

Then, after a while, Sam got angry.

"I don't care if Johnny doesn't come to my party. I hate him, and he's never going to be my best friend again."

Johnny wasn't happy either. He knew he couldn't go to two parties, and he had to make up his mind. So when he was getting ready for bed, he decided to ask his dad.

"Dad, I've got a problem. I promised I'd go to Sam's party on Friday, but now I've been invited to go to Luke's party as well. Luke's party is at Chuck E. Cheese's. My other friends will be there and then they are having a sleepover in tents."

"Hmmm," said Johnny's dad. "You made a promise, and then you got what seems like a better offer. This is a big decision." Then his dad said, "Johnny, what if I got a better offer for a wife? You know, there are a lot of really smart women at my office, and some of them are really friendly."

"You can't do that, Dad," said Johnny. "You made a promise to Mom."

"That's right," his dad said, "and that's why it's really important that we learn to keep our promises, even when we are young."

Early the next morning, Johnny phoned Sam.

"Sam, I'm sorry I upset you by talking about Luke's party. If you still want me to come to your party, I'd really like to come."

Johnny had a blast at Sam's party. In fact, he had so much fun that he didn't even think about Luke's party at Chuck E. Cheese's, and the next morning Sam and Johnny caught a fish that was so big, it took the two of them to pull it in.

A few days later, Johnny got a note in the mail from Sam. It said, "Dear Johnny, thanks for making my party the best one I've ever had." It was the best party Johnny had ever been to as well. Johnny smiled to himself. He felt good inside, and he was so glad that he had kept his promise.

Be a Promise Keeper

The seventh commandment is about keeping your promise through sexual purity both in your mind and in your body. Jesus made it clear that the scope of the seventh commandment includes our thoughts as well as our words: "You have heard that it was said, 'Do not commit adultery.' But I tell you that anyone who looks at a woman lustfully has already committed adultery with her in his heart" (Matthew 5:27–28).

Jesus described the times in which He lived as an "adulterous generation." That means a generation in which many people had become confused in their attitude and disordered in their behavior when it comes to the matter of sex.

We are also living in an adulterous generation. America is a major producer of pornography for the whole world, and we live in an environment where it is extremely difficult to be pure in our minds, in our hearts, and in our behavior. Purity of thought and of life is one of our greatest struggles.

The last thing you want when you are struggling is for someone to yell at you about your failure. What you need is some practical encouragement to show you how you can move forward. That's the purpose of this chapter.

God's Good Gift of Our Sexuality

God created the first man and the first woman. Making them male and female was His decision. That means that God was the first person in the universe ever to have a sexual thought, and that thought was absolutely pure.

In the brilliance of God's creation, He designed two persons to complement each other. God created the woman from the man, taking the rib from Adam, so that when He brought the man and the woman together in the first marriage, it was a kind of reunion for both, and in that union, God placed great pleasure.

This is important, especially for those who may have been brought up with a negative view of sex. The book of Hebrews tells us that "marriage should be honored by all, and the marriage bed kept pure"

(Hebrews 13:4). The reason that it should be kept pure is that it *is* pure. Seeing the purity of God's gift of sexual union within marriage may bring new freedom and joy for some who have been inhibited in this area by a false sense of guilt.

God has given us a beautiful description of the union between a man and a woman in marriage: "A man will leave his father and mother and be united to his wife, *and they will become one flesh*" (Genesis 2:24, emphasis added).

Becoming one flesh is more than a union of two bodies. It is a joining together of two minds, two hearts, and two wills—the partnership of two souls and two spirits. This union begins when a marriage is consummated, but God's purpose is that it should continue, grow, and develop as the marriage matures.

There is a good analogy for this in the way that the Bible describes what it means to be a Christian. When a person is joined in faith to Jesus Christ, he or she is justified. *Justification* is a decisive event by which you are forever bonded to Christ. But that union is only the beginning of your *sanctification,* which is the lifelong process by which you grow in your relationship with Him.

That's how it is with becoming one flesh. It is a decisive event by which you are forever bonded with the one to whom you have given your pledge. But it is also the beginning of a lifelong process of growing together in body, mind, heart, and soul.

Marriages can get into difficulties because some husbands are very interested in being one in body, but they don't have a lot of interest in being one in mind, soul, and spirit. And some wives are very interested in being one in mind, soul, and spirit, but they don't have a lot of interest in being one in body. God has joined these things together, and they should never be separated.

The liturgy used by the Church of England for a wedding service includes a prayer offered by the pastor immediately after the bride and groom have taken their vows, in which he asks that God would "strengthen the union of their hearts by the union of their bodies."

Notice the order: The union of hearts comes first. The gift of sexual union is given to strengthen the love in which it is shared. Our culture has reversed the order. It begins with sex, and then suggests that falling in love will make it better. But God's plan is that the gift of sexual union should strengthen the love that is already shared by a husband and wife in marriage. This gift is neither to be seized outside of marriage nor neglected within marriage.

Living with the Pressure of a Fallen Sexuality

The entrance of sin into the world has affected all of us in every area of life, including our sexuality. The effects of the fall in each of our lives will vary both in their nature and in their degree. We do not all share the same battles, but all of us have some struggles in relation to our sexuality. None of us are yet as God intended us to be.

One of the most common struggles comes when we are tempted to use God's gift of sexuality as a means of finding release or fulfillment, rather than as a means of expressing love. The proper place for sexual union is, as we have seen, in a marriage, which is a lifelong and loving partnership of one man and one woman.

When we take God's gift and use it outside of marriage, either with another person or on our own, then we abuse God's good gift, and we lose sight of its purpose.

The rapid growth of pornography in our time has encouraged many to take sex into a private world in which it is no longer an expression of love, but rather a means of release. In his book entitled, *God's Good Life*, David Field describes sex on your own as the spiritual equivalent of glue sniffing.[1] It's a brilliant analogy. The purpose of glue is to bind two things together. When glue is used for that purpose, it is a marvelous thing. But if a person goes off on his own and uses glue to get high, he is perverting its purpose. That's not what it is for, and if you use it like that, you do damage to yourself.

When sex is reduced to a means of gratification, it becomes a self-serving indulgence rather than an expression of love. The great irony is that when this happens, the gift that God gave for the purpose of deepening a relationship ends up having precisely the opposite effect. Instead of deepening the union, it introduces resentment. It erodes a person's capacity to give, and undermines the very relationship it was designed to strengthen.

If we begin to view sexual expression as an outlet for tension rather than an expression of love, God's good gift will be abused. That can happen even within marriage. God's good gift of sexual union within marriage is abused when it is pursued without love and if it is withheld where there is love.

Christ Has Come to Redeem Our Sexuality

Jesus died to redeem every part of your life, and that includes your sexuality. Being a Christian is not just about saving your soul; it is about redeeming your life.

God's purpose is that every believer will walk in sexual purity. Your body was created by God; it has been redeemed by Christ, and it has become the home of the Holy Spirit. The way that you use your body matters to God. He calls you to honor Him with your body (see I Corinthians 6:20). He wants you to present your body as a living sacrifice to Him, because that is your spiritual worship (according to Romans 12:1). That is why Paul says to Christian believers, "Each of you should learn to control his own body in a way that is holy and honorable" (I Thessalonians 4:4).

God's Commands Are Also His Promises

If all this makes you feel that you are staring failure in the face, let me lead you to the door of hope. Some years ago I came across a wonderful story about a man serving time in prison because he was a thief. Stealing had been his lifestyle until the long arm of the law caught up with him. During his time in prison, he heard the good news of Jesus Christ and was wonderfully converted.[2]

When the time came for his release, the reformed man knew that he would enter a new struggle. Most of his old friends were thieves, and it would not be easy to break the patterns of his old way of life.

The first thing he wanted to do when he was released from prison was to go to church, so on the first Sunday morning of his new freedom, he slipped into a church building and sat down in the back row. As he looked up to the front, the former convict saw the words of the Ten Commandments inscribed on two plaques. Immediately his eyes fell on the words that seemed to condemn him: "You shall not steal."

That's the last thing I need, he thought to himself. *I know my weakness, I know my failure, and I know the struggle I'm going to have with this temptation in the future.*

As the service progressed, he kept looking at the plaque. As he read and reread the words, they seemed to take on a new meaning that he had not seen before. Previously, he had read these words in the tone of a command "You shall not steal!" But now, it seemed that God was speaking these words to him as a promise: "You shall not steal."

He was a new person in Christ, and God was promising that the Holy Spirit would make it possible for him to overcome the habit of stealing. "You shall not steal! You are not going to do this anymore, because you are a new creation and My Spirit lives in you." What once was a condemning command now seemed like a marvelous promise of new possibilities that had been opened up to him by Jesus Christ through that power of the Holy Spirit.

You may be thinking that this story belongs in the next chapter on the eighth commandment, but I'm convinced that many believers need to hear God speaking this seventh commandment to them as a promise: "You shall not commit adultery—not with your body and not in your mind. You're not going to do this, and the reason you will triumph over this temptation is that My Holy Spirit lives in you!"

Cultivate Your Love for Christ

Jesus Christ has come to redeem you, forgive you, restore you, and to lead you on the path of purity. Two strategies will be especially helpful in pursuing this path. The first is to cultivate your love for Christ. The second is to act in the power of the Holy Spirit.

The Old Testament tells us the story of the tempting of Joseph, a young man away from home in a foreign country, where nobody knew him. Joseph was single in Egypt and had landed an upmarket job as the business manager in the household of an extremely rich man by the name of Potiphar.

Potiphar's wife took a liking to Joseph and tried to seduce him. Joseph refused, but Potiphar's wife was not easily discouraged. Day after day she would appear, giving him the eye and trying to entice him. The pressure was relentless.

The Bible records the single strategy that sustained Joseph and enabled him to stand throughout the entire time of this temptation: Joseph said, "How then could I do such a wicked thing and sin against God?" (Genesis 39:9). He called the temptation "sin," and he saw the wound that it would bring to the heart of God.

If you are going to overcome the power of temptation, the first step is to identify the activity to which you are being tempted as sin, and then to see the connection between that sin and the cross of Jesus. Having been redeemed from sin by the blood of Jesus, how could you go back and do this to Him?

Joseph saw that his temptation was not a private issue between himself and Potiphar's wife, or even between himself and Potiphar. It was an issue between Joseph and the Lord.

As long as you are saying that your temptation is no big deal, you will never change. But once you come to the place of saying, "This matters to God so it matters to me," then you will be able to stand even under great pressure.

The strength of your love for Christ will be the key to your triumph over sexual temptation. A new love can be stronger than an old habit. That's why the first step in overcoming the power of sexual temptation is to cultivate your love for Christ.

I'm convinced that most people who struggle with these temptations will find greater help by growing in their knowledge of Christ and the Word among a company of healthy believers than in a group focused on discussing sexual issues.

Your ability to triumph over temptation will depend on the strength of your love for Christ. When that love begins to flourish, you will see your temptation in a new light, and you will be within sight of victory.

Act in the Power of the Holy Spirit

When it comes to your battle with temptation, God does not tell you to pray about it, but to take action against it. The problem with praying about sexual temptation is that you end up focusing more attention on it, and that can have the effect of making the problem worse.

The language of Scripture is always active when it comes to our struggle with temptation. God calls us to put up a fight. We are to "put to death the misdeeds of the body" by the power of the Spirit (Romans 8:13). The apostle Paul reminds us that the grace of God "teaches us to say 'No' to ungodliness and worldly passions, and to live self-controlled, upright and godly lives in this present age" (Titus 2:12).

Many Christians have become confused here and have the idea that they can do nothing in the face of temptation except admit their own helplessness and surrender to the Lord. But the New Testament teaches that God has given us spiritual armor in which we may put up a fight against the wiles of the Devil, which certainly include sexual temptation.

At times during the summer, our family enjoys having lunch on the decking at the back of our home. The problem is that we are often visited by wasps who seem attracted by the food.

Now what do you think we do about that? Does the family join hands in prayer, admitting that we are helpless and asking for deliverance? Of course not. Instead, one of us reaches for the flyswatter or a newspaper. *Whack!* That's the end of the menacing wasp.

That's the language of the New Testament in relation to sin: "Put to death the misdeeds of the body." When you find impure thoughts buzzing around in your mind about that person in the office who shows an interest in you or the adult store that you could visit on the way home or the Internet site that was advertised on your computer, you treat these thoughts exactly like the wasp. You put each thought to death. You cut it off, give it no quarter. Swat it!

If you are a Christian, you have the power to do this because the Holy Spirit lives within you. So don't listen to the Enemy when he tells you that you can't! That's Satan's lie, and if you believe it, you will continue to be bound by his deception. You can overcome this temptation by the power of the risen Lord Jesus Christ that is at work in you. But God calls *you* to act. Put up a fight! Never surrender! The struggle for purity is a lifelong struggle, but you can prevail.

The Struggle to Forgive

Sexual sins are among the hardest to forgive. Hidden secrets and open betrayals bring deep wounds that are not easily healed. It's hard to imagine a pain more acute than that of a man or woman whose spouse has been unfaithful.

If your spouse has lacked tenderness or consideration, used pornography, become involved in an affair, or engaged in some other area of sexual sin, then your spouse faces the challenge of repentance. But it doesn't end there.

When sexual sin has been uncovered, there are always two mountains to be climbed. One person faces the challenge of repenting, and another faces the challenge of forgiving.

Forgiving isn't easy, even when there is true and deep repentance, but your forgiveness, love, and support can play a huge part in healing both your own wounds and the wounds of your spouse.

Churches often choose to deal with sexual issues in the context of a men's retreat. There is nothing wrong with that. But I have become increasingly convinced that the best hope for real change with married folks in this area is found when a husband and wife face these issues together.

If you find that your marriage has been violated by unfaithfulness either in mind or body, the first thing you should look for from your spouse is repentance. If you do not see that yet, pray that it will come, and when it does, ask God to help you embrace it. After all, that's what He does—He forgives as we repent.

If your spouse can repent, you can forgive. God's grace will make both of these things possible. And as your spouse's repentance deepens, so will your forgiveness. There are two struggles here, and the healing of the one can be the healing of the other.

In the story of the Prodigal Son, Jesus gave us a beautiful picture of the healing that comes when repentance meets forgiveness. When the son repents, he begins the long journey back to his father, no doubt wondering all the way how he will be received. But as soon as the father sees his son on the horizon, he rushes out to meet him.

Jesus told this story so that we would know what God is like. He is the Father who meets us in our repentance. God does not stand at a distance from us waiting until our repentance is complete.

When the father sees the son, he goes out to meet him, and then in love, the father brings him the rest of the way home. This is what you can do when God answers your prayers and brings your spouse to repentance.

When one partner in a marriage is ready to break with the patterns of the past and the other is ready to meet his/her mate in their repentance and to walk together the rest of the way home, there is great hope for the future. When repentance and forgiveness meet, healing begins.

Notes

1. David Field, *God's Good Life* (Leicester, England: InterVarsity, 1992), 154.

2. This story also appears in Colin Smith, *Ten Keys for Unlocking the Bible* (Chicago: Moody, 2002). Many people seem to have found it helpful.

"YOU SHALL NOT STEAL."

◆EXODUS 20:15

Am I a taker

or a giver?

eight

Your Struggle
for Integrity

WHEN I READ THE EIGHTH commandment, the first picture that comes to mind is a man climbing out of a window with a mask over his eyes and a bulging sack over his shoulder. And since I have never burgled a house and never felt tempted to do so, my first instinct is to think that this eighth commandment may be one that I have actually kept.

Perhaps you feel the same, though having come this far in our study, you may also have guessed that there's more to this commandment than first meets the eye. The eighth commandment speaks to our struggle for integrity, our attitude toward work, and our battle against laziness and greed.

We've already discovered that each of God's commandments speaks to a whole category of sins. We know this from the teaching of Jesus in the Sermon on the Mount and from the Old Testament, where the whole legal code recorded in Leviticus and Deuteronomy is an exposition of the Ten Commandments, showing the application of each command to particular situations.

The Line of Dishonesty

As we have already seen, it's helpful to think of each command as a railway track with many stations on the line. In the case of the eighth commandment, the line is called dishonesty. At the last station on this line, you will find passengers who would gladly break into other people's property, raid banks, and run massive fraud schemes. Most people will never visit that station, yet all of us have traveled somewhere on this line.

Stealing can be defined as the desire to get as much as possible while giving as little as possible. It is about being a taker without being a giver. On this definition, it is clear that a lot of stealing goes on within marriages, in families, in churches, and in our community.

Every attempt to have much and give little is part of the struggle addressed by the eighth commandment. Let's explore some examples as we apply our definition of stealing to some practical areas of life.

Employees: Giving Full Value

The eighth commandment speaks directly to both employers and employees. It is easy to hear what God has to say to the other side, but we need to make an intentional effort to tune into God's Word for us. If, like me, you are an employee, there is a specific application of the eighth commandment that you need to hear.

Remember, stealing involves trying to get as much as possible while giving as little as possible, and that means that a lot of stealing goes on at work. As an employee, your calling is to give value to your employer.

You earn a living from a person or company who values what you do and pays you to do it. That involves a relationship of trust that you will give value to the person or company that hires you. As an employee, you must regularly ask how you can make your employers feel that they are receiving great value in hiring you.

Whenever you give less than full value to the person or company that employs you, you are stealing from them. Some of the ways in which that can happen include arriving late or leaving early, stretching lunchtimes, or taking extra breaks.

Even when you are working, you can find many ways to rob your employer. These include expanding the work to be done to fill the time available, doing the work that you like and consistently avoiding what you have been asked to do but don't want to, or using work time to pursue your own projects. These are all ways in which an employee can give less than full value to his or her employer, and that is stealing.

Christians need to be especially careful about engaging in evangelism or other forms of ministry during work time. If your employer hired you to do evangelism, there is no problem, but if that is not part of your job description, you need to be very careful. Remember that the way you do your work will be one of the loudest statements about your faith.

One summer, when I was a student, I took a job as a night shift cleaner, working with a team on the David Hume Tower, a large building on the campus of Edinburgh University. The shift ran from ten in the evening until six in the morning, and we had three breaks in the tearoom, as they called it, each night.

Over the summer, I had several opportunities to talk about the gospel. The crew knew that I was a theological student, and that gave them plenty of scope for a wide range of overripe jokes.

After each tea break, the team would spread out over the building, each of us working on a different floor. On one occasion, when I had finished cleaning my floor I decided that I would use the time till the next tea break to read a few pages of a book. I found a corner near one of the windows and soon had settled so deeply into the book that I did not notice the cleaning supervisor creeping quietly into the room.

All he said was, "Is that a good book?" I muttered something about getting finished early, but it was no use. My credibility had just been shot to bits. I had finished my work, but there were other things that I could have done. I could have taken on another task or offered to help somebody else on the team. The cleaning company had not hired me to read a book. I was stealing.

Having a job involves a relationship of trust, and the trust is that you give full value in doing the work that you were hired to do to the best of your ability.

Employers: Paying Fair Wages

The poor may often be tempted to steal from the rich, but it is every bit as common for the rich to steal from the poor. When the Old Testament prophets spoke about sins against the eighth commandment, their primary focus was on the sins of employers and landowners who amassed great wealth but did not share it with the workers who produced it for them.

Scripture speaks directly to tightfisted employers about this scandal: "The wages you failed to pay the workmen who mowed your fields are crying out against you. The cries of the harvesters have reached the ears of the Lord Almighty" (James 5:4).

These workers had toiled hard day after day, breaking their backs to bring in the harvest. They had given full value and brought in a bumper crop. The landowner was enjoying the benefit of this bounty, but he had not shared the rewards of the harvest with those who brought it to him. Instead, he had sent those who made him rich away with scarcely enough to sustain their families. These workers felt cheated. They cried out to God in frustration and anger, and He heard them.

The problem with these tightfisted employers was that they asked the wrong question. They should have asked, "What's the value of my workers?" Instead, they asked, "What's the minimum amount I can get away with paying?"

Employers face the temptation of trying to get as much as possible while giving as little as possible, and that is stealing. God will hold Christian employers responsible for their stewardship in paying appropriate salaries to those who generate the wealth they enjoy.

Alongside the issue of fair payment, there is the troubling issue of late payment. Paying your bills on time is a Christian responsibility both privately and in business. The apostle Paul says, "Give everyone what you owe him: If you owe taxes, pay taxes; if revenue, then revenue; if respect, then respect; if honor, then honor" (Romans 13:7).

If you owe money on a bill and you don't pay it, or if somebody gives you a loan and you don't repay, that is stealing. It is no use saying, "Well, they don't need the money." That's not your business. Your responsibility is to pay what you owe. It is part of integrity, and that is the basis of trust.

Traders: Charging Fair Prices

Price gouging is another example of breaking the eighth commandment. False weights and measures were often a problem in Old Testament times (Deuteronomy 25:13–15; Amos 8:5). The modern equivalent would be what we call "overpricing goods and services."[1] That's just one more example of trying to get as much as possible while giving as little as possible.

Another way in which this can happen is by cutting the quality of your work. If you are providing a service, your customer will often not know the corners you can cut or the materials you can substitute to make the job easier or more profitable for you.

You may be tempted to settle for a job that is "good enough" for the customer, knowing that if you were doing the same job for yourself, you would do it better. That is stealing.

Your customer is paying you for this work and has trusted you to do it. Your calling is to provide the best value to your customer for a fair price.

Owners: Giving Due Credit

Another area in which many are tempted to steal involves taking what belongs to another person and reproducing it as if it were your own.

Material that has been placed under copyright belongs to the person or people who created it. Reproducing what belongs to another person as if it were your own is called plagiarism. Schools enforce severe penalties for students who do this, and it is a totally unacceptable practice for politicians. But strangely it is not unknown for pastors to reproduce other people's material from their pulpits!

When students use quotations and ideas in their school papers, they need to credit the sources in endnotes. If they lift huge portions—or the entire paper—from one or two sources, they're stealing ideas and words. The preacher, teacher, trainer, technician, or designer who uses material that has appeared elsewhere should also give credit to the source. Otherwise, he or she is stealing words and ideas.

Then there is the whole issue of copying computer software or music CDs that belong to a friend so that you don't have to buy the product yourself. That is stealing. You are taking what the artist or company has produced without giving the return to which he, she, or they are entitled and would receive if you purchased their product.

Sometimes when I've made this point, I have been told, "The artist doesn't really need it." That's probably true, but it's not the point. Think it through: If you say that it is acceptable to steal from someone who has much more than you do because you think that they have enough already, that would mean that most people in the world have the right to steal from you. Millions of people in the world own much less than the average high school student in America.

Integrity means paying what you owe. It means doing your own work rather than taking someone else's and presenting it as if it were yours.

Christians: Showing Total Commitment

If stealing is about trying to get as much as possible while giving as little as possible, then the eighth commandment speaks powerfully to the way that many believers approach the Christian life.

A rich man once asked Jesus, "What must I do to inherit eternal life?" He wanted to know the minimum requirement for entering into heaven. His desire to receive eternity's blessings at the minimum price revealed a deep problem in his heart. He wanted to gain much and to give little. That's breaking the eighth commandment.

The Dignity of Work

He who has been stealing must steal no longer, but must work, doing something useful with his own hands, that he may have something to share with those in need.—Ephesians 4:28

God wants you to stop stealing and to replace a lifestyle of laziness and greed with one that is marked by hard work and generosity. The New Testament makes it clear that this is how we are to fulfill the eighth commandment.

The word that Paul uses for "work" here literally means "to labor to the point of fatigue." So if you know what it is to fall into bed at night feeling absolutely spent because of the demands of your work, you've experienced what Paul is talking about here. You have labored to the point of fatigue, and Paul says that this is a good and worthy thing. Indeed, this is what God is calling you to do.

Work is God's good gift, and the Bible takes a positive view of working hard. This was one of the distinguishing marks of Paul's ministry: "I worked harder than all of them," he wrote (I Corinthians 15:10). Others in the early church wanted an easy life in ministry, but Paul labored and struggled. These words reflect what authentic ministry looks like. It is hard work.

The effort Paul put into his work was a mark of honor. Indeed, the hardworking pattern of his life became a model for other believers. "In everything I did," he says, "I showed you that by this kind of hard work we must help the weak" (Acts 20:35).

Working for the Lord

The Bible commends the value of working hard, and that includes approaching your work with a positive attitude: "Whatever you do, work at it with all your heart, as working for the Lord, not for men" (Colossians 3:23). No matter how menial or exalted a task may seem, believers are to regard their work as something that is offered directly to the Lord, and we are to make sure that we always offer our best.

Learn to love your work and to value it as a good gift from God. Do not look at it as a necessary evil that you have to endure in order to get money. View it as a God-given opportunity to contribute. Give thanks to God for your work and for your ability to do it. If you are employed, thank Him that somebody values what He has enabled you to do so highly that they would pay you money to do it for them.

Your work is God's means of providing for you and helping you to grow. Over time you may find that you outgrow your work. If that happens, it is another cause for thanksgiving. Having grown through your work, you are now ready for God to lead you to the next assignment. Always remember that the best way to prepare for what God wants you to do tomorrow is to offer your best in what He has called you to do today.

Offering your work as worship to the Lord will give you a

whole new perspective on your job, even if that work seems dull and unimportant.

I have been thinking about the wide variety of jobs that I've done over the years, from high school, through college, and up to the present time. They include being a grocery store assistant, night-shift cleaner, houseparent to mentally handicapped children, and pastor.

Question: In which of these jobs was I working for the Lord? Answer: All of them.

We often make the mistake of creating a huge chasm in our minds between what we call "sacred" and what we call "secular." We do this because we feel certain that God is interested in prayer, preaching, and evangelism, but we are not quite so sure that God is interested in microcircuits, school lunches, and grocery store checkouts.

Of course He is! That's one of the first things that we learn in the Bible. God gave Adam the work of naming the animals and then entered into that work by bringing the animals to him. God wants to participate in your work too.

That's how it will be in God's marvelous new creation. In heaven, you will discover the joy of doing exactly what God designed you to do with fulfillment and freshness for all eternity. God's purpose is that you will experience a foretaste of heaven on earth as you offer your work as worship to Him.

When you begin to think of your work in this way, it will change your attitude and raise the quality of all that you do. Your work will take on new meaning and significance, and you will discover a new joy.

Contributing to the Needs of Others

He . . . must work . . . that he may have something to share with those in need.—Ephesians 4:28

We fulfill the eighth commandment not only by working but also by giving. God wants you to contribute to the lives of others, and you can do that both by the way you work and by the way you use what you earn. Once you see that giving is the reason for working, the artificial barrier between paid work and volunteer work will soon disappear.

I regularly enjoy hearing my wife's stories from her work as a teacher of young children. One day the discussion in her class was about what each of the children would like to do when they grew up. One little girl had it all mapped out. "First," she said very deliberately, "I'm going to be a secretary. Then I'm going to be a nurse. Then I'm going to be a mother, and then I'm going to be a teacher."

"Well, you are going to be very busy!" Karen said.

"Yes," responded the five-year-old, "and the sooner I get started, the sooner I can retire!"

If you think of work as something you do in order to build a big enough pile of money to be able to retire, you've completely misunderstood the biblical vision of work. The purpose of life is that we contribute. Retirement may mean the end of your paid work, but it does not mean the end of your usefulness. As long as you have life, God has work for you to do.

God has given each of us time, talent, and treasure. You have been trusted with the Holy Spirit and with gifts for ministry. How are you using what He has given to contribute to the lives of others?

In explaining the eighth commandment, the Heidelberg Catechism makes it clear that stealing includes "all squandering of our gifts." Jesus told a story about three servants who were trusted with talents. Two of them invested what they had been given. The other buried what had been entrusted to him in the ground (Matthew 25:14–18). That is stealing.

Take a look at the gifts, talents, and resources that God has given to you. If you squander these gifts, you are stealing from God by failing to use what He gave for the purpose He intended, and you are stealing from other people by withholding from them what God intended them to receive through you.

Wherever you go and whatever you do, you have a God-given contribution to make to the lives of other people. Cultivate the habit of looking to see what you can bring to the lives of other people. Whenever you engage in a conversation, or sit down for dinner with your family, try to see what contribution you can make, and ask God to help you make it. If you have to attend a meeting at work, watch out for what you can bring to the discussion. Don't check out and let the conversation go on around you. There is a reason for your being there, so make your contribution.

Givers and Takers

Fulfilling the eighth commandment involves a radical change of heart in which you move from being a taker to a giver. Instead of grasping much and giving little, you begin to give much and grasp little. That is what it means to fulfill the eighth commandment.

Satan is the great taker of what does not belong to him. He is "the thief [who] comes only to steal and kill and destroy" (John 10:10). He is constantly trying to get as much as possible while giving as little as possible. Those who do his work will find their efforts bring diminishing returns.

In contrast, Jesus said, "I have come that they may have life, and have it to the full" (John 10:10). Satan is the great taker of what does not belong to him. Christ is the great giver of all that He owns.

Christ turns takers into givers. The gospel is more than good advice; it is good news. It is not a set of instructions on how to change. It is a new dynamic of life in which you become a giver because the Spirit of Jesus lives in you.

Pour out your life for Him and you will have no regrets. When you receive your reward, you will not be disappointed. In the presence of Jesus you will not be asking if it was really worth it. Standing before Him in awe, you will wonder why you found it all so difficult.

Note

1. James Packer makes this point in his discussion of the Ten Commandments in *I Want to Be a Christian* (Eastbourne, England: Kingsway, 1977), 225.

"YOU SHALL NOT GIVE
FALSE TESTIMONY AGAINST
YOUR NEIGHBOR."

◆EXODUS 20:16

Can my words

be trusted?

nine

Your Struggle
with Truth

EVERY WEEK, THE BRITISH prime minister faces a thirty-minute trial by fire as he answers questions in the House of Commons. The atmosphere in the chamber is electric for this weekly slugfest. Creative jabs, biting sarcasm, and one-line put-downs flow freely in the cut and thrust of parliamentary debate.

In contrast to the more sedate atmosphere of debate in the United States Senate, the British Parliament, as it's known in Britain, is brutal. But one thing a member of parliament can never do is to call another member a liar. Any use of the words "lie," "lies," or "liar" with reference to another member of parliament would lead to immediate expulsion of the member making the accusation from the chamber. Calling someone a liar is deeply offensive.

Of all the struggles we experience in relationships, the challenge of forgiving someone who has lied to you is surely the hardest. Lies are the Devil's native language (John 8:44). Perhaps that's why deception leaves such ugly scars.

The good news is that God cannot lie (Titus 1:2). Truth is written into His nature. He will not deceive you or mislead you. He is the one person in the entire universe you can trust absolutely.

God gave the ninth commandment because He wants His people to be like Him: truth-tellers and worthy of trust. He wants you and me to deal in truth rather than lies, in precision rather than distortion, and in honesty rather than deception.

Strictly speaking, the ninth commandment addresses the issue of perjury; that is, standing up in court and making an accusation that you know isn't true. That's what happened when Jesus was arrested and brought to trial. False witnesses, who wanted to have Him crucified, were prepared to say whatever was necessary to achieve their desired result.

But the scope of the ninth commandment reaches far beyond our words in a courtroom. As we have already seen, God's commandments are like a railway track with many stations on the line. The ninth commandment is about the line of lying. Perjury in a court of law is a station at the end of the track. You may never have been at that station, but you have certainly traveled on the line.

Stations on the Line of Lying

The essence of lying is saying something that will achieve a desired result without regard to whether it is true. There are many ways in which this can happen. Take *flattery* as an example: Someone has described flattery as "saying to someone's face what you would never say behind his or her back!" Flattery happens when you want to make a good impression, so you say what you think another person wants to hear even if that bears little relation to reality. Flattery doesn't sound as bad as perjury, but it is a station on the line of lying.

Exaggeration is another station on the line. In your attempt to make an impression, you overstate what you said, did, or accomplished, taking credit that really belongs to someone else. Or, if you are looking for sympathy, you may overstate the wrong that was done to you because you want the person who hears your story to feel sorry for you. Telling your story in a way that misleads a person by hiding or excluding what they would need to know to make a balanced judgment is a form of lying.

Gossip is another station on the line of lying. This involves passing on news about another person that may or may not be true with the intent of harming that person. The lie may be in your words or it may be in your motive; passing on information under the pretense of being helpful when your real aim is to alter perceptions about the other person.

Someone has likened gossip to ripping a feather pillow open on a windy day. Once the feathers are out, there is no way to gather them back.

The reason that we are prone to lying is that we are more deeply committed to ourselves than we are committed to the truth. Truth is hard for sinners because it never puts us in a pure light. Somewhere deep inside the human heart, there is an instinct that makes us want to hide from the truth. We like to think of ourselves as seekers after truth. In reality, our first instinct is to run from it (Romans 3:11).

There is a great moment in the film *A Few Good Men* when in the heat of cross-examination in a military court, an attorney played by Tom Cruise shouts, "I want the truth!" The colonel, played by Jack Nicholson, explodes in anger: "You can't handle the truth!" That's our problem.

The Broad Road of Deception

The Bible makes it clear that the entire human race has fallen into the grip of a lie. The whole Bible story is about the unfolding and the final exposing of this massive deception that began with one lie in the garden of Eden and will end with the destruction of all liars in the lake of fire (Revelation 21:8). At the center of this great drama is Jesus Christ who says, "I am . . . the truth" (John 14:6).

Every lie, deception, or distortion (personal, professional, or political) in the history of the world can be traced back to the activity of Satan. Jesus described him as "a liar and the father of lies" (John 8:44). All lies reflect his character.

Satan's odyssey of lies began when he lost touch with reality and conceived the notion that instead of him serving God, God should, in fact, serve him.

This massive self-deception caused him to be thrown out of heaven, and when God placed the first man and woman in the garden, Satan's great desire was to involve them in his delusion. His aim has never changed.

From the Garden to the Jungle

Satan's first strategy was to question God's truth. "Did God really say, 'You must not eat from any tree in the garden'?" (Genesis 3:1).

Many are still asking Satan's question: Can you *really* know what God has said? Undermining confidence in the Word of God set the stage for Adam and Eve's rebellion. If a person can't be sure about what God has said, how could he or she be expected to put it into practice? Losing confidence in God's Word is always the prelude to departing from it. That's why displacing and discrediting the Scripture has always been Satan's first strategy.

The doubt and confusion generated by Satan's lies were obvious when Pontius Pilate was asked to pass judgment on Jesus. Pilate asked Jesus many questions, and Christ answered plainly. "For this reason I was born, and for this I came into the world, to testify to the truth. Everyone on the side of truth listens to me" (John 18:37). It was an astonishing claim. Jesus made it clear that His words were the truth and that the first evidence of a person dealing in truth is that they follow His teaching.

Pilate's response was terse: "What is truth?" (18:38). Pilate was a politician. He knew that people would say anything to get their way, and he had come to the conclusion that what people call "truth" is only a way of speaking about what they want.

In this case, a large and restless crowd had gathered outside Pilate's home and wanted Jesus dead, so Pilate handed Him over to the guard and they led Him away to be crucified. It was the ultimate miscarriage of justice.

Where truth falls, justice follows. A man who believes that truth is nothing more than a personal perspective or opinion cannot bring justice. Judgments can only be made if there is an objective truth to judge.

The reason that God will be able to make a final judgment about all of us on the last day is that there is an objective truth about you and me, and God knows it completely. He knows the truth about you better than you know it yourself. He sees mixed motivations when we have turned a blind eye to them, and He sees the work of His Spirit in our souls when it is hidden from us.

Loss of confidence in the existence of truth is the single most destructive force in our postmodern society. Perhaps we are experiencing a reaction to arrogant and overconfident truth claims in the past. That would be a good thing. We all have much to learn about humility, and we must make sure that we do not confuse truth with our own opinion or endorse our own ideas with God's name as if they were His. Confident assertions of what God has not revealed and evasions of what He has revealed are both examples of putting ourselves in the place of God.

But to question or deny the existence of truth by reducing it to a matter of perspective or opinion is disastrous. If we cannot know the truth, no one can be expected to tell the truth. And if truth is merely opinion, then it cannot be tested because there is no objective standard by which you can measure a personal opinion.

In such a world nothing could be pronounced "right" or "wrong." Justice would be replaced with a legal system that would exist only to make a "decision" that would itself be nothing more than another opinion backed by the power of the state.

Ultimately the loss of truth leads to a society in which the most powerful opinion wins. That's the law of the jungle. That's what Satan does: By questioning the reality of truth, he takes us from the garden to the jungle.

Powerful Delusions

The biggest problem with a lie is that it keeps you from the truth. Years ago, I visited a lady who was suffering from delusions. She had been a member of my congregation for many years and had been admitted to the hospital after suffering for some time with a severe mental illness. She was convinced that she was the Antichrist and that the mark of the Beast was on her forehead. She pointed to her forehead, but there was no mark to be seen.

I will never forget the frustration of trying to tell her the truth, knowing that she was in the grip of an illness that was causing her to believe a lie. Believing a lie excludes the truth.

When people found Jesus' teaching hard to understand, He explained without apology that the problem was not with the teaching but with the hearing. "Why is my language not clear to you? Because you are unable to hear what I say" (John 8:43).

Paul tells us that "the god of this age [Satan] has blinded the minds of unbelievers, so that they cannot see the light of the gospel of the glory of Christ" (2 Corinthians 4:4).

With blindfolds over human eyes and earmuffs over human ears, the only way that any of us is going to see and hear the truth is if someone comes to release us from the power of the deceiver. It is going to take someone who can raid the kingdom of darkness, take off the blindfolds, remove the earmuffs, and then bring us from the darkness of delusion into the light of truth. That is why Jesus Christ came into the world. The entrance of His Word gives light and brings life.

New Life Through God's Word

God creates the capacity for hearing the Scriptures through Scriptures. The light of God's Word opens eyes that did not see, and the truth of His Word opens ears that did not hear. God's Word is the living seed that brings that new life into being. "You have been born again, not of perishable seed, but of imperishable, through the living and enduring word of God" (1 Peter 1:23).

Think about the way in which physical life begins: The living seed comes, and in a secret, mysterious, and wonderful way new life is conceived. Not every seed leads to new life, but the new life never happens without the seed.

The miracle of conception is instantaneous. In a moment, hidden within the woman's body there is a new life, and the amazing thing is that she may not even be aware of it. The next day she may go to work, and it seems as if everything is exactly as it was before. But a few weeks later, she begins to feel that something is changing inside her. She does not feel as she felt before, and she begins to wonder if she could be pregnant.

That's how new life begins in the physical sphere, and Peter wants us to know that it happens in the same way in the spiritual sphere. The living seed of God's Word comes, and in a secret miracle of grace, the Holy Spirit plants it within your soul.

No wonder Satan hates the Word of God. If he can lure the church away from the Bible, he will be well pleased. So the pressure will always be on pastors to become entertainers, counselors, administrators, and anything else except preachers and teachers of the Word of God.

Faith comes by hearing, and hearing comes through the Word of Christ (Romans 10:17). The Word creates the capacity for hearing, and that hearing will lead to faith. I think that we need to recover our confidence in this simple strategy for ministry in the church. If we want to see new life, we have to plant the seed from which it comes. Where that seed is planted, and watered with our prayers, there will be a harvest.

That's why so many people come to faith in Christ through Bible study groups. The entrance of God's Word gives light. The power of the delusion is broken by the truth.

Living the Truth

There's more to embracing the truth than believing the words of Jesus. Large crowds followed Jesus because they believed Him and enjoyed His teaching. John records that "to the Jews who had believed him, Jesus said, 'If you hold to my teaching, you are really my disciples. Then you will know the truth, and the truth will set you free'" (John 8:31–32).

These are challenging words to people who had already affirmed that they believe. Jesus wants them to know what this truth can do in their lives and how that is going to happen. Christ challenges those who say they believe to "hold" to His teaching by obeying it and putting it into practice. When that happens, Jesus says, they will know the truth and the truth will set them free.

At first sight this seems the wrong way around. It would seem more natural for knowing the truth to come first, and for obeying to follow, but Jesus insists that among people who profess to believe, the order is the other way around. It's as we put His truth into practice that our knowledge of it will grow and we will experience its power in our lives.

The importance of this order came home to me recently in hearing the story of one person's journey to living faith in Christ. "I was brought up going to church," she said, "and as far as I can remember I always believed, but it didn't make much difference in my life. Then one day something happened, and I had to *forgive.*"

She paused as the pain came back fresh to her memory. "I didn't want to do it," she said. "I couldn't do it, but I knew that if Jesus had forgiven me, then I had to forgive, and I knew that the only way I could forgive was if He did it through me. So I decided to forgive, and that was when what I had always believed became real for me in a whole new way."

Her story demonstrated the pattern of Jesus' teaching. *Believing* that leads to *obeying* results in seeing and *releasing*. Real change never comes simply by saying that you believe. It begins when you hold to Jesus' teachings; that is, when you put them into practice.

When you take a step of obedience, Jesus promises that two things will happen. First, "you will know the truth." What seemed cloudy and distant will become clear and personal. It will be in you, and it will be true for you. Second, "the truth will set you free." Things that bound you will bind you no longer. Things that you could not do before will become possible for you.

Jesus spoke about this when He told a story about two men who heard the Word of God (Matthew 7:24–29). Imagine these two men in the same church listening to the preaching on Sunday morning. Picture them as members of the same small group sitting around a table with their Bibles open.

Both men receive the same teaching, and both of them believe it. Looking at these two men, you can't tell much difference between them. They both seem pretty smart, successful, and generally on top of their game. In fact, there is only one difference between these men: One hears the Word *and puts it into practice,* and the other does not.

Somewhere in the course of life, both of these men will face a storm, and when that happens the difference between them will become obvious. According to Jesus' story, the man who hears the Word and puts it into practice will be like a house built on the rock. The storm rages around it, but the house stands firm. But the man who heard the Word and did not put it into practice will be like a house built on the sand. When the storm comes, it will collapse because it has no foundation. Which of these men best represents you?

Professing to believe is of little value if your believing is not translated into obeying. Taking a step of obedience will put you on the path to seeing and releasing.

Truth Terrorists

Obeying the ninth commandment means speaking the truth to your neighbor, but what does that look like in practice? Does speaking the truth mean that you have to share everything you have experienced with other people? Does speaking the truth mean that you have an obligation to tell another person everything you ever thought about them?

Some Christians are confused about what is appropriate when it comes to speaking the truth. Others abuse the truth and become "truth terrorists." A terrorist is a destroyer, and a truth terrorist is someone who uses the truth to destroy. These terrorists come in two varieties: one who opens up the truth in a way that is naïve, and the other who uses the truth in a way that is brutal.

The naïve variety is well illustrated in a story my father-in-law once told me. Early in his career as a musician, he was invited by one of his colleagues to join a group of friends who had decided to pursue a psychological experiment. The single rule of the group's meetings was that everyone would speak the truth, the whole truth, and nothing but the truth.

My father-in-law had no interest in such a group and told his colleague that he regarded the idea as extremely dangerous.

He was right. The group began with five couples. One of the wives in the group was a doctor who happened to be stunningly attractive. So with a commitment to tell the whole truth, it wasn't long before several men in the group began to share some of their thoughts about her, which led their wives to share other thoughts about her too.

You can imagine what happened. Within a year, every one of the marriages in that group had ended, including the doctor's. She ended up with another member of the group. The truth had been used to bring destruction.

The problem here is naïveté. Some of the truth about you and me is ugly, and the only place to go with that is to the cross and the blood of Jesus. Sharing the poison in you openly will only spread the infection. Each of us has a responsibility to discern what we should share, with whom, when, and why.

In his book *Encouragement: The Key to Caring,* Larry Crabb deals with building authentic relationships. Here's part of what he wrote in the chapter "Total Openness: The Wrong Solution":

> I am persuaded that one of the key culprits responsible for the lack of self-control is our cultural emphasis on the desirability of self-expression. Our values revolve too much around ideals like openness, authenticity, transparency, assertion, fulfillment, and genuineness. And we tend to neglect as outdated, concepts like sacrificial giving, self-discipline, self-denying love, obedience, and willing endurance.
>
> As our energy has been directed more toward *expression* than *restraint,* we have suffered a slow steady erosion of our ability to commit ourselves to any direction that runs counter to our urges. . . .
>
> Any group of people, whether married couples, friends, church staff, or Bible study groups, will run into serious trouble if they emphasize self-disclosure and emotional expression as premium values.[1]

That's a powerful and much-needed warning from a respected Christian counselor. When self-expression becomes more important than Christ-centeredness, it will not be long before there are significant problems. So it is important to measure the appropriateness of what we share. Paul gives us the working principle for that discernment. "Do not let any unwholesome talk come out of your mouths, but only what is helpful for building others up according to their needs, that it may benefit those who listen" (Ephesians 4:29). Use truth for building up, not for tearing down.

The Brutal Truth

The second type of truth terrorist is the one who uses the truth to blast other people in confrontation or even in evangelism. Some people love confrontation and use the truth as a reason to have more of it. "I just told him the truth," they say as they explain with pleasure how they gave another person a piece of their mind. The problem here is not naïveté, but brutality.

Our calling is to speak the truth in love (Ephesians 4:15). That means that I am to speak the truth in a way that will be in the best interests of the hearer. So there will be times when I have to exercise courage and say what someone does not want to hear, and there will be other times when I need to exercise restraint and hold back what a person is not yet ready to hear. There is a time to confront and there is a time to conceal.

The truth terrorist does not understand this. He (or she) comes in with all guns blazing and uses the truth as an excuse for unloading in a way that can be quite brutal.

One Sunday, during my first year as a pastor, a visitor came to the church I was serving in London. He was a keen Christian involved in full-time ministry and was passing through town. He was on his own, so I invited him for lunch after the service. Over the lunch table he tore my sermon to shreds and unloaded a critique of the church, which I would describe as substantial!

He justified this use of the one hour that he spent in our home on the basis that we are called to speak the truth. Looking back, I have to tell you that some of the things he said were true. But they were neither kind nor appropriate.

If Jesus Christ had revealed to you everything that was wrong in your life on the day that you were converted you would have been completely devastated. But He didn't do that—and He doesn't do that. He leads us gently, one step at a time.

So watch out for the truth terrorists. Practice speaking the truth in love. Don't expect a new Christian to learn in one week what God taught you in ten years. Learn to weigh the effects of what you say in the light of the trust you have earned. "Let your conversation be always full of grace, seasoned with salt, so that you may know how to answer everyone" (Colossians 4:6).

Note

1. Larry Crabb and Dan B. Allender, *Encouragement: The Key to Caring* (Grand Rapids: Zondervan, 1990), 42–43.

What's drawing

my heart?

Your Struggle

for Contentment

THE TENTH COMMANDMENT is the key to understanding the other nine. All of the other commandments are about specific actions. Murder, adultery, stealing, and perjury are all behaviors that can be seen, but the tenth commandment is different. It deals with what happens in the secret place of your heart.

Coveting is known only to you and to God. My neighbor would know if I stole his car, but he would never know if I coveted his car. Nobody knows your secret desires, thoughts, or fantasies, but the tenth commandment makes it clear that they matter to God.

Many Christians have the idea that God was only concerned with outward actions in the Old Testament and that Jesus put a new spin on the commandments, applying them to the attitudes of our hearts.

"You have heard that it was said to the people long ago, 'Do not murder, and anyone who murders will be subject to judgment.' But I tell you that anyone who is angry with his brother will be subject to judgment. . . . You have heard that it was said, 'Do not commit adultery.' But I tell you that anyone who looks at a woman lustfully has already committed adultery with her in his heart." (Matthew 5:21–22, 27–28)

The reason that Jesus taught as He did is that the Ten Commandments are about inward attitudes as much as outward actions, and the tenth commandment makes it clear that this was the original intent of God when He gave the commandments to Moses.

This is why we have used the picture of each command being like a railway track with many stations down the line. Each command speaks not just to one sin but to a whole category of sins, and these sins are not just in our words and actions; they include the secrets of our minds and hearts.

The tenth commandment makes it clear that God calls us to more than upright behavior. He is calling us to purity of heart, not just that you should *do* right but that you should *be* right.

This is an important insight for sharing the gospel with our Jewish and Muslim friends. One of the reasons we often find communicating the gospel difficult is that we live with this mistaken idea that the Old Testament is concerned with outward conformity, and that the New Testament is concerned with matters of the heart.

We wrongly assume that Jews and Muslims, who are committed to the Old Testament, are only interested in moral codes, when, in fact, the Old Testament itself calls us to a spiritual life that is only possible through the power of God's Holy Spirit.

The Problem for Morally Upright People

The problem for morally upright people, whether Jews, Muslims, or Christians, is that they find it very difficult to *feel* that they need a Savior. After all, if a person has gained a good education, raised a stable family, run a successful business, gone to church, given generously to people in need, never committed murder, adultery, or perjury, and never robbed a bank, what would such a person need saving from?

It is natural for morally upright people to see their religion as something that they offer to God, which taken along with the rest of their lives should put them in a position to enter eternal life.

So when the preacher talks about sin and the need to be forgiven, we are glad to hear it because we believe this, and we know that it is a good message for many people, but it can sometimes seem distant from us.

If that's where you are today, my prayer is that God will speak to you through the tenth commandment. That's what He did for two men in the Bible who were awakened to their spiritual need by this commandment. The first was a man who is often referred to as the rich young ruler. I'm going to picture him in the twenty-first century and call him "the man who was living the American dream."

Living the American Dream

Here's a profile of our man living the dream: He is voted most likely to succeed when he graduates high school. He plays sports at college, graduates cum laude in business, and marries the following year. He achieves his goal of a six-figure salary early in his thirties, pays off his mortgage in his forties, and shifts his attention from success to significance in his fifties. He sees the world in his sixties and plans to retire in his seventies.

This man knows that life is more than money; it is also about values, and values are important to him. He has raised a good family. He has been a great husband and father. He is known for his generosity to others. More than that, he is a true believer in God; he knows that beyond death lies eternity, and he wants to make sure that he is ready. So he has set the goal of living a good life: He attends church, he prays to God, and he gives generously to good causes.

Then one day, the man who is living the American dream hears that Jesus is in town. So he comes to Jesus and asks, "What must I do to inherit eternal life?" (Luke 18:18).

I can picture this man with his leather Day Timer open, ready to write down the answer. "Give me the checklist," he is saying. "I'm up for a challenge, and I'm ready to do whatever You say needs to be done. Give it to me straight, because I want to make sure that I've covered my bases."

Jesus says to this man, "You know the commandments: 'Do not commit adultery, do not murder, do not steal, do not give false testimony, honor your father and mother'" (verse 20).

I can picture this man checking off these commands in his mind. *"Do not commit adultery"—that's the seventh commandment; I'm OK there. "Do not murder"—that's the sixth commandment. Well, I know I'm in the clear there. "Do not steal"—that's number eight; no problem with that one. "Do not give false testimony"—that's number nine; no problems there.*

Now what else did He say? Oh, yes, "Honor your father and mother"—that's the fifth commandment, and there are no problems for me there either.

Then he thinks to himself, *This is great! These are the things that I have been doing all my life, so I'm obviously on the right track.* So he tells Jesus: "All these I have kept since I was a boy" (Luke 18:21).

Notice that the one commandment Jesus did not mention was the tenth. I have no doubt that this was intentional, because what Jesus does next is to apply the tenth commandment with devastating effect: "You still lack one thing. Sell everything you have and give to the poor, and you will have treasure in heaven. Then come, follow me" (verse 22).

Jesus uses the tenth commandment to identify the single greatest struggle of this man's life. His outward conduct is morally upright, but his inner attitudes are centered on himself. The whole of his life is about pursuing what *he* wants to achieve. Even his morality is a means to the end of eternal life, which is just one more item on the checklist of what he wants to accomplish.

Peer and Fear

People may live a moral life for reasons that have little or nothing to do with loving God or neighbor. Indeed a large part of what we call morality is influenced by the *peer factor* and the *fear factor.*

I have often thanked God that my sons have had good friends, especially during their teenage years. Every parent wants their kids to have good friends, and the reason is that we all know a large part of our children's behavior will reflect the behavior of their friends. But what kind of morality is that?

If we were to do a survey of the men in my church, I doubt that we would find many who pray five times each day. But if we lived in Saudi Arabia, where Muslim men traditionally pray five times a day, we would probably do the same—not because we love God more, but simply because that's what everybody else does! It's the peer factor.

Peer factor morality doesn't bring you any closer to God because it does not arise from love but from conforming to what everyone else is doing. God calls us not just to do right but to be right, and that means that He is looking for something deeper than actions that reflect the behavior of other people around us.

Alongside the peer factor, a large part of your morality may have been shaped by the fear factor. Perhaps, like the man who was living the American dream, you could go through a checklist of the Ten Commandments and feel that you come out looking pretty good. You have never robbed a bank, murdered, or committed adultery. But why not?

Is it that your heart has been filled with a deep love for God and for other people, or is it simply that the risks were too great? Sometimes the reason that we do not steal, lie, or commit adultery has more to do with fear of the consequences for our position and reputation than it has to do with a deep desire to do what is right.

It is your thoughts that reveal the real condition of your heart. Your secret thoughts reveal what you would do if you thought you could get away with it. These thoughts are the measure of who you really are.

The tenth commandment raises disturbing questions for morally upright people. If Christianity were simply a program for promoting good moral behavior, then all that would matter is that we do the right things. But God calls us not just to do right but to be right, and that means that morally upright people are sinners too.

The Killer Commandment

The New Testament tells us about another man whose deeply moral life came unglued when he understood the tenth commandment. His name was Saul of Tarsus. We know him better as the apostle Paul.

Paul fit the same profile as the rich young ruler. He was born into a successful and well-connected family, received a marvelous education at the school of Gamaliel, and was set on the track of a distinguished career.

For much of his life, he saw himself as a morally upright person committed to keeping God's Law. Looking back on his earlier perspective, he wrote, "If anyone else thinks he has reasons to put confidence in the flesh, I have more: circumcised on the eighth day, of the people of Israel, of the tribe of Benjamin, a Hebrew of Hebrews; in regard to the law, a Pharisee; as for zeal, persecuting the church; as for legalistic righteousness, faultless" (Philippians 3:4–6).

Later in his life, Paul had a new understanding of the Ten Commandments, and a different evaluation of himself in the light of them.

"I would not have known what sin was except through the law" (Romans 7:7).

For many years, this man had looked at the commandments and concluded that he was morally upright. Now he tells us that the commandments showed him that he was a sinner. What made the difference?

The answer is the tenth commandment. "I would not have known what coveting really was if the law had not said, 'Do not covet'" (Romans 7:7). Paul is saying, "Here I was with my moral checklist, thinking that I was doing well. Then one day, I came face-to-face with the tenth commandment."

"The commandment came," he says, describing a specific experience in his life (Romans 7:9). We don't know if this was before or after the Lord appeared to him on the Damascus Road, but whenever it happened, Paul tells us that the tenth commandment forced him to reevaluate his position before God. Suddenly it dawned on him that God was not looking only at his outward actions but also at the inner desires and motivations of his heart. The tenth commandment nailed him. It strangled the life out of his self-righteousness.

The tenth commandment is the killer commandment for morally upright people. And once you have grasped the meaning of this commandment, you will soon see that you are a long way from keeping the other nine.

Two men in the New Testament were confronted by the tenth commandment, and they had completely different responses:

- The rich young ruler walked away from Jesus with great sadness. No doubt he found another spiritual teacher whose message fit his lifestyle and made him feel more comfortable.
- The apostle Paul saw the hollowness of his own morality, and he embraced the tough message of his failure before God's Law. That led him to Christ and to a new life (Galatians 3:24).

Perhaps you are like the man who was living the American dream, or even like Saul of Tarsus. You work hard, show integrity, and are known to be trustworthy and generous. You have good values, and you see your religion as something that you offer to God. You try to follow the Ten Commandments as your moral code, and your biggest problem is that your moral uprightness keeps you from seeing that you need a Savior.

The tenth commandment is for you. You need the killer commandment. It will show you that morally upright people need a Savior. Pastors and preachers need the tenth commandment. Sunday school teachers and missionaries need the tenth commandment. Without it we might soon become arrogant, self-righteous, smug, and patronizing. But if we grasp the tenth commandment, we will feel that we need the Savior as much today as on any other day of our lives and as much as the most despicable person we could imagine.

Those who know this will be marked by deep humility and by a heartfelt love for Christ. A man who feels that he is moral will never love Christ deeply. But a man who feels his desperate need of a Savior will offer his whole life in love and in gratitude to Christ.

The Problem of the Heart . . . the Heart of the Problem

Martyn Lloyd-Jones was a medical doctor who became a great Bible preacher. He often used his medical training in diagnostics to explain what the Bible teaches about the human condition.

"Sin," he wrote, "is not merely a matter of actions and of deeds; it is something within the heart that leads to the action. . . . What we must really concentrate upon is not so much sins as sin. Sins are nothing but the symptoms of a disease called sin and it is not the symptoms that matter but the disease, for it is the disease that kills, not the symptoms."[1]

Murder, adultery, stealing, and lying are symptoms of a disease called sin that lies in the human heart. Symptoms of the disease vary, and they can often be suppressed. What matters most is not the symptoms you are showing but the disease you are carrying. The change that God wants to bring into your life is more than a modification of your behavior. It is a change of your heart. Christ did not come to deal with your symptoms. He came to deal with your disease.

I love the story about a man who regularly prayed at length in his church prayer meeting. He used some quaint phrases, and somewhere in his prayer he would often say, "Lord, clear the cobwebs from our mind."

Week after week he did this. Eventually, at one meeting, someone got up and prayed, "Oh, Lord—just kill the spider."

King David understood this when his life was derailed after he indulged in an affair with a woman called Bathsheba. David had covered it all up, but God broke the cover, speaking to David directly through the prophet Nathan.

This brought David to repentance and led him to write Psalm 51, where he confessed his sin and asked God to wash him, cleanse him, and forgive him. But he didn't end there. He asked God to create a pure heart and a right spirit within him (Psalm 51:10). "Lord, I need You to deal not just with what I did, but with the heart that made me do it," David was saying. "If You forgive this sin, but You don't change my heart, it won't be long before I find myself doing the same thing all over again. I need more than forgiveness. I need You to change my heart. I am asking for more than medicine to relieve the symptoms; I need the Great Physician to heal my disease."

There are many ways to change a person's behavior. If all you want to do is to stop drinking or break free from some other compulsive habit, you don't need Jesus to do that. You can do it with some good therapy, accountability, and an effective support group. There are many ways to deal with the symptoms, but only Christ can deal with the disease.

The heart of the human problem is the problem of the human heart. That's why the great question is not so much how to change your behavior, but how to change the heart that gives rise to that behavior in the first place.

New Life in the Power of the Spirit

Throughout this study, we have seen that God's commands are also His promises through Jesus Christ, and this tenth commandment holds a marvelous promise in the power of the Holy Spirit: "You shall not covet."

Coveting is chasing the wind; it is a life of always seeking but never finding. Christ offers to deliver you from the power of coveting. "Come to me, all you who are weary and burdened, and I will give you rest," He said. On another occasion, Jesus declared, "If anyone is thirsty, let him come to me and drink. Whoever believes in me, as the Scripture has said, streams of living water will flow from within him" (Matthew 11:28; John 7:37–38).

He offers a life in which you will not be bound by a relentless compulsion to achieve the next goal. You will not be duped by the illusion of finding satisfaction in the next thing that you gain.

You shall not covet. You can experience such a change of heart that instead of relentlessly chasing the wind, you can learn to be content as you find in Christ what is of supreme and lasting value (Philippians 4:11).

This is far deeper than a change of behavior. It is a change of heart. You do not need to be trapped in a life where you are never content because you are always longing for the next thing. The fruit of the Spirit from this last commandment is formed over time. It will grow slowly, but it will transform your life.

More than Forgiveness

I have met many people whose grasp of the Christian faith is limited to forgiveness and the Law. They understand that Christ died on the cross for our sins and that, as a result, we may be forgiven. They also understand that Christ calls us to follow His commandments. So their idea of Christianity is that we do our best to follow the Law and ask for forgiveness when we fail to live up to this standard.

Forgiveness and the Law can deal with our symptoms, but they cannot deal with our disease. Forgiveness deals with the consequences of what we have done, but it does not deal with the source. Forgiveness and the Law cannot deal with the fundamental problem of our sinful nature.

The gospel is more than forgiveness and the Law. It is a new nature and a new life. When you come to faith in Jesus Christ, God puts His Spirit within you. That's His promise. "I will give you a new heart and put a new spirit in you. . . . I will put my Spirit in you and move you to follow my decrees and be careful to keep my laws" (Ezekiel 36:26–27).

The Holy Spirit will bring you back to the Ten Commandments. The first evidence of His presence in your life will be that you have a deep desire to please God and to serve Him by being a channel of His love into the lives of others.

This will be the greatest struggle of your life, and so before you set out on this journey, you need to know if it's possible. The Heidelberg Catechism faces this issue head-on:

> Q. *Can those converted to God obey these commands perfectly?*
> A. *No. In this life, even the holiest have only a small beginning of this obedience. Nevertheless with all seriousness of purpose, they do begin to live according to all, not only some, of God's commandments.*[2]

I've found this answer to be profoundly helpful. No Christian is everything that God calls him or her to be. The finest Christian you have ever met has only a small beginning of obedience.

But there *is* a beginning of true holiness in every believer. No Christian is completely pure, but there is the beginning of purity in every Christian. No Christian is completely content, but there is the beginning of contentment in every Christian. What we have now is a beginning of truth, of peace, of integrity, of rest, and of worship;

we truly "begin to live according to all, not only some, of God's commandments."

Every day of your Christian life offers opportunities for the new life that God has begun in you to grow stronger. And when you stand in the presence of Jesus, what He has begun in you will be complete.

Notes

1. Martyn Lloyd-Jones, *Studies in the Sermon on the Mount* (Grand Rapids: Eerdmans, 1984), 237.

2. The Heidelberg Catechism (Grand Rapids, CRC, 1975), Question 114.

Study Guide

THIS STUDY GUIDE is ideal for personal study or as part of a regularly scheduled group discussion, whether at home or church. For group study, this guide is designed for use in ten sessions. Read one chapter of this book, and then prepare your answers to the questions that follow before the group meeting.

Please note that sentences shown in boldface in each set of questions come directly from the corresponding chapter in the main text. They are emphasized both to show their importance and to help you locate them in the corresponding text.

Our prayer for you is that in this material you will recognize these ten great struggles in your own life and by God's grace cultivate a growing love for Him and other people.

Your Struggle
with God

1. Think back over your life and identify one person whose directions or instructions you *gladly* followed. Maybe it was a pastor, teacher, coach, or a parent: _____

   What, in particular, made you want to follow them?

   _____

   _____

2. **The God you worship will shape the values you hold, and the values you hold will shape the lifestyle you choose.**

   Name a lifestyle decision you are currently thinking about:

   _____

   Take the two options you are considering and trace them back to the values behind them. Then trace the values back to the object of your worship.

   Option: _____

   Value behind it: _____

   Object of worship: _____

   Option: _____

   Value behind it: _____

   Object of worship: _____

Write down your observations:

_____

_____

3. **This attempted reshaping of God is not new. It goes all the way back to the garden of Eden.** God had told the first man and woman not to touch the Tree of the Knowledge of Good and Evil. But Satan wanted them to make a different choice. His **goal** was to change how they *behaved*. His **strategy** was to undermine what they *believed*.

    Satan's strategy sought to undermine three *areas of belief*:

    #1—*Did God really say . . . ?*
       (How can you be sure you have the *correct interpretation?*)

    #2—*You will not surely die.*
       (This talk about *death* following sin is surely *exaggerated.*)

    #3—*You will be like God. . . .*
       (You can *decide* your own *values.*)

    Which area of belief is most difficult for you? (Give an example.) Why?

    Area: _____ Example: _____

    Why? _____

    _____

4. You are dependent. You depend on food, air, and water. But God depends on no one. He exists in the power of His own eternal life. **He is God whether you believe Him or not.** He is who He is. So to make Him your God is to come in line with reality.

    Place a check mark on the line below that best represents your orientation to God:

    hatred_____   avoidance_____   love_____

Try to identify or describe the *primary reason* for your current orientation:

_____

_____

5. God introduces Himself by saying: "*I am the LORD your God,* who brought you out of Egypt, out of the land of slavery." If God were to deliver the Ten Commandments to you personally, today, how do you think He would introduce Himself to you?

    Write in your own words what you think He would say:

    _____

    _____

6. The Creator, who has all power and is accountable to nobody but Himself, does not make His appeal to you on the basis of raw power, like a dictator. Instead He says, "I am the LORD your God, who brought you out of Egypt, out of the land of slavery" (Exodus 20:2). It is on the basis of His unconditional grace, mercy, and love that He appeals to His people to follow His commands.

    You will never be ready to embrace God fully until you are convinced that He is good. We may submit to raw power, but we can never love raw power. How convinced are you that God is good?

    $\longleftarrow$ _____ $\longrightarrow$

    not at all   circumstantially   unconditionally

    Explain why you placed the *x* where you did: _____

    _____

7. There is all the difference in the world between a kidnapper and a lover. A kidnapper may say, "You are mine" on the basis of power. A lover says, "You are mine" on the basis of affection. **Imagine the risen Lord Jesus Christ holding out His hands that were pierced with nails, and saying, "I am the Lord your God. I gave Myself to deliver you. Don't put any other gods before Me."**

    When you hear Jesus' appeal, what does it sound like to you?

    Like a kidnapper (power) ____ Like a face in the crowd (weak) ____
    Like a lover (affection) ____

What part of His appeal most influenced your placement of the *x*? Why?

_____

_____

8. Let these applications of the first commandment stimulate your thinking:

   a. *Baby Step: Cultivate your affection for God.* (Choose one or more to concentrate on this week.) Pursuing a life of loving loyalty to God means cultivating your affection for Him. As with any relationship of genuine love, it involves thinking about Him, appreciating Him, honoring Him, desiring Him, fearing Him, trusting Him, hoping in Him, delighting in Him, calling upon Him, and giving thanks to Him.

   b. *Substantial Move: Turn away from all that offends God.* (Evaluate this list and turn away from anything you find here.) I've found it helpful to identify some of the sins that break the first commandment: pride, hero worship, infatuations, allowing other people to bind your conscience, superstition, consulting the Devil, mediums, fortune-tellers . . . impatience with God . . . teaching or believing that all religions lead to God . . . despair.

   c. *Radical Life-Change: Embrace the Lord unconditionally.* When Jesus said "follow Me," none of the disciples knew where that would lead, and you can't know that either. Making Christ Lord of your life could get you into some tough situations. It might lead you to the other side of the world. It may even cost you your life. But God is calling you to a step of commitment based on trust, because you know that He is God and that He is good.

   As you reflect on the applications above, write below how you would like to respond to God's words to you in the first commandment:

_____

_____

_____

chapter two

Your Struggle

with Worship

1. Did any of the following play a part in your religious experience growing up: icons, beads, pictures of Jesus, religious paintings or sculptures, or a crucifix with Jesus on it? If so, how do you believe it may have shaped your understanding of God?

   _____

   _____

2. **God is greater than your highest thought about Him.** You cannot reduce Him to a system of logical thought. You cannot confine Him to the narrow boundaries of your experience. Nothing in creation can represent the Creator.

   Which are you more inclined to do?

   ❑ Try to reduce God to a system of logical thought
   ❑ Try to confine Him to the narrow boundaries of my experience

   We know Him not by cultivating our imagination, but by believing His revelation. When might your inclination (identified above) tend to *complement* ("supplement") His revelation, and when might it *eclipse* it?

   complement: _____

   _____

   eclipse: _____

   _____

3. Saint Augustine said **idolatry is worshiping what should be used or using what should be worshiped.** Try and rewrite this in your own words.

   _____

   _____

4. **The way to dethrone created things that could become idols is to ask what they are for.** Describe what you believe is _the purpose_ of each of the following:

   • Marriage _____

   • Family _____

   • Money _____

   • Work _____

   • Church _____

5. **God is not some impersonal force that exists to fulfill your fantasy. He is who He is,** and any attempt to make Him conform to what we want Him to be is utterly offensive. Loving God means embracing Him as He is.

   What are some ways we can protect our love for God by guarding ourselves against this human tendency to make God conform to what we want Him to be?

   _____

   _____

   _____

6. **Jesus is the one true image of the invisible God.** He is the exact representation of God's being (Colossians 1:15; Hebrews 1:3). That is why Jesus could say, "Anyone who has seen me has seen the Father," (John 14:9).

   Nothing created can lead you to the Creator. But you can come to God through Jesus, in whom God has drawn near to you. If you will embrace Him, He will embrace you, and that is where eternal

life begins. Do you agree or disagree with these statements? Why or why not?

_____

_____

7. **Let God be "I AM WHO I AM" and some will call you intolerant, arrogant, or even a bigot.** But others will consider the words of Christ and because of your declaration and the Spirit's power believe the no-holds-barred words of Jesus: "I am the way and the truth and the life. No one comes to the Father except through me" (John 14:6).

Have you ever been called intolerant, arrogant, or a bigot because you declared the uniqueness of salvation through Christ? What happened?

_____

_____

What do you think they meant by it when they called you by that name?

_____

Have you ever led someone to Christ by declaring Jesus' unique message? What happened?

_____

8. Reflect on these "next steps." How might God be calling you to respond to the second commandment?

   a. _Baby Step: Admit to God that I am using Him._ (Confess this to God and to another Christian you trust and ask them to pray for you.) Something within me wants to use God more than I want to worship Him. I want Him to forgive my sins. I want Him to get me into heaven. I want Him to give me good health, long life, an intimate marriage, success in my career, healthy children, and multiple grandchildren. The list is unending, and if I find that I go without one of these things, I am tempted to find fault with God.

   b. _Substantial Move: Take steps to dethrone an idol in my life._ (See question 4.) Make plans to shift your relationship with this idol in order to dethrone it.

c. *Radical Life-Change: Begin praying in submission to God's will.* (Stop praying primarily as a means of asserting your own will.) We are never in more danger of seeing God as a resource to be used than when we come to Him in prayer. Somewhere deep in our hearts lurks the idea that if God really loves us, He is under an obligation to give us what we ask and that if we ask in faith, He really owes it to us to come through. That's idolatry. Prayer is not a tool for manipulating God. True prayer is offered in the name of Jesus Christ, and that means that it can only be offered in submission to His will.

As you reflect on the applications above, write below how you would like to respond to God's words to you in the second commandment:

_____

_____

_____

Your Struggle
with Religion

1. **The way that you use a person's name says a great deal about what you think of them.** Think of a positive and a negative example of this truth:

    positive: _____

    negative: _____

2. **Big names cause people to sit up and take notice.** Identify a celebrity "name" that causes you to sit up and take notice. What impressions do you associate with it?

    name: _____ *impression(s):* _____

    _____

3. The name of God is used in support of claims that are so obviously contradictory that **a growing number of people have given up hope of knowing any truth about God at all.**

    As you think about the many competing truth claims about God, put an *x* on the continuum below that best represents how you would finish this statement: *I believe . . .*

    ◄───►

    | None are | There must be | No way of knowing; | Many roads |
    | true. | one true story. | what is truth? | lead to God. |

    Why did you locate it where you did?

    _____

    _____

4. Misusing the name of God is also an issue within the church.

Empty—Sadly, the highly publicized cases of misusing God's name are too often mirrored in Protestant churches where leaders who bear the name of Christ behave in ways that have made His name profoundly unattractive to many.

Frivolous—One of the defining marks of our time is that *God is now weightless.* . . . He rests upon the world so inconsequentially as not to be noticeable.

Presumptuous—The most common misuse of God's name among evangelical believers is the presumptuous way in which we often claim God's direct guidance by announcing that "the Lord led me," or "the Lord told me."

When you talk to family, coworkers, or neighbors, do their attitudes about God or the church reflect any of the above problems? Give an example:

_____

_____

5. Take McDonald's as an example. One day, I decide to get creative so I start thinking: *McDonald's is a wonderful Scots/Irish name, but there's nothing distinctively Scottish about the menu. So why don't I do something about it? Instead of the Big Mac, I can serve up haggis burgers. Then for breakfast I can offer oatmeal, and instead of coffee I can serve hot mugs of tea.*

You can't use the name McDonald's to endorse your own thing, and you can't use the name of God like that either. What item(s) do you think belong on the menu of someone who bears the name "Christian"?

_____

_____

_____

6. "You shall not misuse the name of the LORD your God, *for the LORD will not hold anyone guiltless who misuses his name"* (Exodus 20:7, emphasis added). The third commandment points directly to two New

Testament Scriptures that speak about a sin for which there is no forgiveness. Jesus said: "I tell you the truth, all the sins and blasphemies of men will be forgiven them. But whoever blasphemes against the Holy Spirit will *never be forgiven;* he is *guilty of an eternal sin*" (Mark 3:28–29, emphasis added).

This statement has troubled many people who wonder if they may at some time have committed this unforgivable sin. Do you ever wonder about this?

_____

The Bible does not teach that anyone who misuses the name of God, Jesus, or the Holy Spirit will inevitably/automatically go to hell. But it does teach that unless you make the right use of God's name you will not go to heaven. Try to write this statement in your own words:

_____

_____

7. **God's answer to a world that blasphemes His name is a community who honors His name.** "All day long my name is constantly blasphemed. *Therefore my people will know my name*" (Isaiah 52:5–6, emphasis added). Honoring the Lord's name is our highest calling. Christ will be honored when the world sees a community of people who show awe and affection for Him.

   How do you reflect to the world an *awe* of God?

   _____

   _____

   How do you reflect to the world an *affection* for God?

   _____

   _____

8. **If you are a Christian, you bear the name of Christ and the reactions of many people to God's name will be informed by what they see in you.** Let these applications of the third commandment stimulate your thinking:

a. *Baby Step: Stop using God's name as a vulgarity.* If you have gotten into the pattern of saying "Oh my God," or "good God" every time you are surprised, ask for God's help to overcome the habit, and ask a good friend to hold you accountable as you make the change.

b. *Substantial Move: Leave room for testing what God has said and a place for listening to other believers who also have the Holy Spirit.* We should be very careful about using God's name as an endorsement for an idea that could in time turn out to be a mistake. It is more honoring to Christ, and more fitting to the spirit of humility, to say "I *believe* that the Lord has led me," or "I *feel* that the Lord has directed me," when describing our experience of guidance.

c. *Radical Life-Change: Turn away from a life of using the name of God in your own way or for your own ends.* "Many will say to me on that day, 'Lord, Lord, did we not prophesy in your name, and in your name drive out demons and perform many miracles?' Then I will tell them plainly, 'I never knew you. Away from me, you evildoers!'" (Matthew 7:22–23).

As you reflect on the applications above, write below how you would like to respond to God's words to you in the third commandment:

_____

_____

_____

chapter four

Your Struggle

with Time

I. **The overfilled plate of our lives leaves us unable to walk freely, and we often feel that we are just one step away from disaster.** Identify what's on your plate:

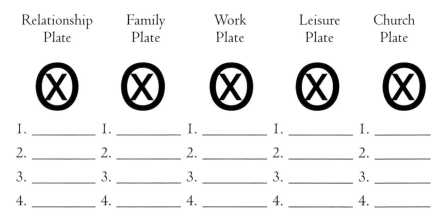

Relationship Plate	Family Plate	Work Plate	Leisure Plate	Church Plate
1. _____	1. _____	1. _____	1. _____	1. _____
2. _____	2. _____	2. _____	2. _____	2. _____
3. _____	3. _____	3. _____	3. _____	3. _____
4. _____	4. _____	4. _____	4. _____	4. _____

2. **Some Christians have thought that they were honoring God by making Sunday the dullest day of the week, a day marked by long lists of things that you could not do, rather than a day of delight.**

Growing up, how did you typically experience Sundays—as a day at church?—a day to sit in front of the TV?—a day just like every other? —or something else?

_____

Did you look forward to it? Why or why not?

_____

_____

3. **God could have made the world in an instant, so why did He choose to make the world in six days?** The answer would seem to be that God was modeling a pattern of how we should divide our work. "Six days you shall labor and do all your work . . . for in six days the LORD made the heavens and the earth, the sea, and all that is in them" (Exodus 20:9, 11).

The successful worker will be one who learns the ability to divide the work and establish priorities. Write down what you need to accomplish in one area of your life—then break it down.

area: _____ What needs to be accomplished:

_____

_____

Let's break it down. What needs to be accomplished . . .

this *year?* _____

this *month?* _____

this *week?* _____

tomorrow? _____

4. "Six days you shall labor and do all your work" (Exodus 20:9). **Divide your time as God did, and you will be able to enjoy completing your work.** At the end of each day, God saw that His work was good. You don't find God saying, "I've made the moon and the stars, but I haven't gotten around to the fish and the animals, and I'm nowhere near starting on the man!"

Instead, God enjoyed His completed work at the end of each day.

a. Think back over your last week of work—how much did you enjoy it?

←——————————————————————————————→

almost no satisfaction ___ occasionally satisfying ___ great personal satisfaction ___

Too often, I feel burdened by what I have to do tomorrow more than I find pleasure in what God enabled me to do today.

b. Think back over your last week of work—how would you describe the effects of worrying about what you needed to do tomorrow?

⟵————————————————————————⟶

minimal _____   debilitating _____   overwhelming _____

Do you believe your work should be satisfying and enjoyable? Why or why not?

_____

_____

5. **Rest is the enjoyment of completed work. That's what God did on the seventh day.** "He rested on the seventh day. Therefore the LORD blessed the Sabbath day and *made it holy*" (Exodus 20:11, emphasis added). God calls us to follow His pattern by keeping the Sabbath day holy. The word *holy* means separate or different, not bound up with the rest. So God is calling us to make one day different from the rest of the others so that we can savor the joy of what has been completed.

Spend some time thinking about what a Sabbath day for you (or you and your family) might *include* and what you would *exclude*. (If you are married and/or have older kids, discuss this with your spouse and/or children.)

include: _____

exclude: _____

Are there further resources you would need to actually do this? What are they?

_____

_____

6. "Therefore the LORD blessed the Sabbath day and made it holy" (Exodus 20:11). God's pattern of resting on the seventh day reminds us that we can enter into rest only when we have completed our work. We do not rest in order that we will be able to work; we work so that we will be able to rest.

It is an anticipation of the day when all our work will be complete and God's people will celebrate together in the full splendor of His immediate presence. **The Sabbath is a window in time to strengthen your grip on eternity.**

Brainstorm ideas for bringing the eternal implications of the Sabbath into focus:

---

7. We cannot rest until our work is done. **If I cannot finish the work of keeping God's commandments, how can I hope to enter into God's rest?** It would be possible only if someone else completed the work for you, and that is precisely what Jesus Christ has done. That is why Jesus is able to say, "Come to me . . . and I will give you rest" (Matthew 11:28).

Have you experienced this kind of rest? Are you experiencing it now?

---

8. **Christ's finished work sets me free to offer my work as a loving expression of gratitude and worship, flowing out of the rest that I find in Him.** How would God have you respond to the fourth commandment?

   a. *Baby Step: Divide up your work and set priorities for a month.* (Build on your work from question 3.) The successful worker will be one who learns the ability to divide the work and establish priorities.

   b. *Substantial Move: Help someone enjoy the blessing of the Sabbath.* Some people have responsibilities from which it is very difficult to rest. I'm thinking especially of single parents, those who care for the elderly, or parents of special-needs children. It takes a community to make it possible for folks with unrelenting responsibilities to enjoy the blessing of the Sabbath.

   c. *Radical Life-Change: Provide the means of rest for those in your sphere of influence.* "The seventh day is a Sabbath to the LORD your God. On it you shall not do any work, neither you, *nor your son or daughter, nor your manservant or maidservant, nor your animals, nor the alien within your gates*" (Exodus 20:10, emphasis added).

How did the applications above stimulate your thinking? Write below how you would like to respond to the fourth commandment:

_____

_____

How would you need to realign your values to be obedient to God in this area?

_____

_____

_____

Your Struggle
with Authority

1. The first people God puts in the path of your life are your father and your mother. **Parents are the first authority figures in our lives.**

   What one thing are you thankful for in your relationship with your parents?

   _____

   _____

   What one thing have you struggled with in your relationship with your parents?

   _____

   _____

2. **Your first experience of a person with authority will shape your reaction to other authorities.** If, in your early experience, you saw parental authority used well, you will most likely have an instinctive respect for people who are given authority in other areas of life. But if you experienced the abuse of authority, you may find that you are instinctively suspicious of other authorities, and that where you en-counter authority, you want to resist it and establish your independence from it.

   How do you typically respond to authority? Write down a couple of examples of people in authority over you, and describe how you have responded to them.

   Example: _____ *Response:* _____

   _____

Example: _____ *Response:* _____

---

3. The fifth commandment would be easy if it said, "Honor your father and mother *as long as they are honorable.*" But God's Word doesn't say that. He puts certain people in our way, and some of them are difficult to honor.

    He does not allow us the luxury of choosing who we should honor. Identify a situation you are facing or have recently faced (let the scenarios below stimulate your thinking), and write down what goes through your mind as you consider honoring this person.

    a. You are a Christian student and find yourself in class with a difficult teacher.

    b. You have a difficult boss who behaves dishonorably or unethically.

    c. You feel your pastor or elders are leading the church in an inappropriate way.

    Situation: _____

    Feelings: _____

    Barriers: _____

    Excuses: _____

    Other: _____

4. **[God] puts certain people in our way, and some of them are easy to honor. With others it is extremely difficult.**

    Where have you seen God's authority best represented?

    _____

    _____

    Where have you seen God's authority most distorted?

    _____

    _____

5. **The greatest challenge for any parent is to consider how you are representing God in the life of your child.** (This is also true in any other position of authority we hold.)

a. **Wisdom**—Wisdom can tell when your child is being a wild donkey, and when he or she is like a bruised reed. Discern the difference and then you will know how to use your strength.

b. **Sufficiency**—The healthy parent and the effective leader is the one who finds his or her sufficiency in God and therefore is free to serve those God has placed in their care. A parent who has not fulfilled their own hopes and dreams can easily slide into living them out through their children. A father or mother who has not felt loved may try to find what they lack in their child.

c. **Love**—Authority without love is always destructive. This is especially important for Christian parents. Sometimes, we can long so deeply for our children to follow Christ that we run the risk of manipulation. Love woos but it never forces, and a wise parent will discern the difference.

Reflect on your own exercise of authority. In light of the three boundaries above, where do you think you are the strongest? Where are you weakest? Why? (Try to be as specific as you can.)

Strongest: _____ *Why?* _____

_____

Weakest: _____ *Why?* _____

_____

6. **A wise father once said to his son, "If I ever have to choose between being your father and your friend, I will always choose the role of your father. You have many friends, but you only have one father."**

Do you agree with this statement? Why or why not?

_____

_____

7. **"We must never be too direct in this matter** [making a decision for Christ] **especially with a child; never be too emotional. If your**

child feels uncomfortable as you are talking to him about spiritual matters, or if you are talking to someone else's child and he feels uncomfortable, your method is obviously wrong. . . . You are bringing pressure to bear. That is not the way to do this work."

Do you agree with this statement? Why or why not?

_____

_____

8. Here are some ideas to stimulate your thinking about how you could respond to the fourth commandment:

    a. *Baby Step: Make God's Word your primary parenting resource.* Of all the materials that are available on parenting today, there is no greater resource than the Word of God. Learning who God is will give you the ultimate template for parenting. Think of all the ways in which you stand in the place of God for your child. You are the child's guardian, provider, shepherd, intercessor, teacher, and example. What your child experiences from you will shape that child's impressions of God.

    b. *Substantial Move: Pray for yourself and for your parents.* If your parents are still in that position [unworthy of honor], you may feel alienated from them. But even if the relationship has broken down, you can still ask God to give you compassion for them. Pray that God will give them what they lack. That's the Spirit of Jesus: He does not treat us as our sins deserve.

    c. *Radical Life-Change: Take your eyes off your parents' failures.* If you have suffered through abused authority, you may have feared the authority of God, and therefore kept at a distance from Him. But the healing of many wounds will begin as you look away from the failings of your parents and up into the face of God. Maybe you are wondering where you can find the wisdom, sufficiency, and love that you need for parenting your children. The answer is that you will find all these things in God Himself. He is our wisdom, and He is completely self-sufficient, the great I AM.

    How did the applications above stimulate your thinking? Write below how you would like to respond to the fifth commandment:

    _____

    _____

Your Struggle
for Peace

1. **The reason that human life is so valuable is that it bears the image of God.** The offense involved in taking a human life is that it involves destroying the image of God. "You shall not murder" (Exodus 20:13).

   Describe in your own words what it means to be made "in the image of God."

   _____

   _____

2. "Whoever sheds the blood of man, by man shall his blood be shed; for in the image of God has God made man" (Genesis 9:6). In these words, God made it clear that there is a vast chasm between the life of fish, plants, and animals and the life of a man or a woman who is made in God's image.

   Many people today have lost sight of that chasm. Where do you see evidence of this in our culture today?

   _____

   _____

3. When discussions about the sixth commandment get going, two controversial issues usually come up. One is the issue of war, and the other is capital punishment. Christians have held different positions on both of these issues, and there is room for legitimate debate on both between people who are serious about applying the teaching of the Bible.

I'm convinced that there are some situations in which if a life or lives are taken, many other lives may be saved. Do you agree or disagree? Why?

_____

_____

4. "You shall not murder" (Exodus 20:13).

   a. God forbids acts of *murder*. This would involve taking the life of your neighbor, whom God calls you to love.

   b. The sixth commandment speaks to the issue of *abortion*, which is taking the life of an unborn child.

   c. The sixth commandment also speaks to the issue of *euthanasia* in our society. Euthanasia involves making a decision that a person's life is no longer worth living and that some action should be taken to end it.

   d. Another application of the sixth commandment is the issue of *suicide*; that is an attempt to take your own life, which has been made in the image of God.

   Have you ever struggled with one of these areas? If so, how did you decide?

   _____

   _____

   Which of the neighbors above do you believe our society has the hardest time loving: the one who murders, aborts a child, practices euthanasia, or commits suicide? Why do you think this is the case?

   _____

   _____

5. Jesus makes it clear that **the scope of this commandment goes far beyond acts of murder, and that it searches out the thoughts and attitudes of our hearts.**

Jesus taught that abusive speech is a direct violation of the sixth commandment. We might call this rudeness, but Jesus makes it clear that it is a station on the line of conflict and that language that is rude, insulting, abusive, or demeaning is a violation of the sixth commandment.

If angry words that insult or diminish another person are a violation of the sixth commandment, then all of us are guilty. Put an *x* on the line below where you believe your position is, based on the sixth commandment:

I plead	the jury is	innocent until
no contest! _____	still out _____	proven guilty _____

Explain why you placed the *x* where you did:

_____

_____

6. God calls you to love your neighbor *as yourself,* and that means that He wants you to take good care of your own life and your health. You are a steward of the life that God has given you. It is of unique and irreplaceable value, so handle your own life with care.

   You can break the sixth commandment by neglecting a proper pattern of sleep, by addiction to work, by an improper use of food, drink, or drugs, or by a lack of proper exercise. Evaluate your thinking about the stewardship of your own life:

These things don't	I have "nagging" concerns	I take these
"really" matter _____	about these things _____	things seriously _____

7. When Christ explained the meaning of the sixth commandment, He applied it by saying that we should **settle our disputes as quickly as possible** (Matthew 5:25). This theme runs throughout the New Testament.

   Are you involved in a dispute with someone? What has been your approach to this conflict?

waiting for them	hoping it will	settling it
to take the first step _____	just "go away" _____	as quickly as I can _____

8. Consider the following applications of the sixth commandment:

   a. *Baby Step: Steward your body.* You can break the sixth commandment by neglecting a proper pattern of sleep, by addiction to work, by an improper use of food, drink, or drugs, or by a lack of proper exercise.

   b. *Substantial Move: Settle a dispute.* The principle is clear: If there is a way to settle a dispute with integrity, take it. That's what God wants you to do. Jesus is the Prince of Peace. He is able to bring peace into the deepest wounds of your life.

   c. *Radical Life-Change: Embrace the life God gives you to the full.* Look over the following suggestions. Choose one to stimulate your thinking. Develop plans to embrace the life God has given you more fully. Share your plan with someone who knows you well and will encourage you to pursue this.

   - *Ask God to give you a vision of what your life can be.* Take a couple of hours alone every week for the next couple of months to pray and ask God to give you a vision for your life. Keep a journal of this time with God for future reference.
   - *Seize every opportunity to develop yourself.* Identify an area of personal development that you or someone else has rejected as "too selfish" or "not important enough." Begin gathering info to take a first step in this direction.
   - *Look for ways you can be a good steward of all the gifts God has given you.* Read Matthew 25:14–30. What investment(s) can you make this year (or over the next five) that will multiply the talents God has given you for His kingdom?
   - *There is no greater way to embrace life than to begin a relationship with Jesus Christ.* [Jesus] said "I have come that they may have life, and have it to the full" (John 10:10). Talk to a Christian friend or pastor, and ask them to help you get started with this new life.

   How did the applications above stimulate your thinking? Write below how you would like to respond to the sixth commandment:

   _____

   _____

   _____

Your Struggle
for Purity

1. **The seventh commandment is about keeping your promise.** Think about your life and the people who have kept their promises to you. Choose one person and try to describe some of what it must have cost for them to keep their promises to you:

   people: _____

   one person: _____ *the cost:* _____

   _____

2. **The best message I ever heard on the seventh commandment was given to a class of elementary-age children in our church.** The Sunday school teacher was launching into a story that has stayed in my memory ever since. It's about a boy called Sam and his friend called Johnny.

   ❏ Johnny loved Chuck E. Cheese's. (*competing loves*)
   ❏ He found that his other friends were all going to Luke's party. (*opportunism*)
   ❏ He had promised to go to Sam's party, but now he felt like he wanted to go to Luke's. (*feelings*)

   Look again at Johnny's thinking as he considers breaking his promise to Sam. Which one of the reasons is *the strongest pull for you* when you struggle with keeping your promises? (Place a check mark in the box.) Identify a specific time when you struggled with this.

   _____

   _____

3. **"You made a promise, and then you got what seems like a better offer."** Consider the words of Johnny's father to his son:

> "Johnny, what if *I got a better offer* for a wife?
> You know, *there are a lot of really smart* women at my office.
> *Some of them are really friendly."*

Now consider Johnny's response:

> "You can't do that, Dad.
> *You made a promise* to Mom."

Why is it so much *easier* for Johnny to see that breaking a promise is wrong for his dad? Why is it *harder* for us to see this in our own lives?

_____

_____

4. The entrance of sin into the world has affected all of us in every area of life, including our sexuality. The effects of the fall vary in each of our lives, both in its nature and in its degree. We do not all share the same battles, but all of us have some struggles in relation to our sexuality. None of us are yet as God intended us to be.

One of the most common struggles comes when we are tempted to use God's gift of sexuality as a means of finding release or fulfillment, rather than as a means of expressing love. *Contrast* what you think it means to use God's gift of sexuality to express love with what it means to use this gift as a means to finding release or fulfillment:

_____

_____

5. **If all this makes you feel that you are staring failure in the face, let me lead you to the door of hope.** The first thing he wanted to do when he was released from prison was to go to church, and so on the first Sunday morning of his new freedom, he slipped into a church building and sat down in the back row.

Put yourself in the converted thief's shoes. Would you . . .

❏ Feel condemned?

❏ Sit through the service feeling defeated?
❏ Get up and walk out?

What would have given you hope?

_____

_____

6. The Bible records the single strategy that sustained Joseph and enabled him to stand throughout the entire time of this temptation: Joseph said, "How could I do such *a wicked thing*, and sin against God?" (Genesis 39:9, emphasis added). He called the temptation sin, and he saw the wound that it would bring to the heart of God.

    If you are going to overcome the power of temptation, the first step is to identify the activity to which you are being tempted as sin. Try to remember the last time you were tempted sexually—put an "x" in the place that best represents your attitude about it:

    ← _____ →

    it's no big deal   I know it matters to God,   this matters to God,
                              but it doesn't matter   and it matters to me!
                              as much to me

    Then [you need] to see the connection between the sin and the cross of Jesus. What connection do you see between sexual temptation and Jesus' cross?

    _____

    _____

7. Jesus gave us a beautiful picture of the healing that comes when repentance meets forgiveness in the story of the Prodigal Son. When the son repents, he begins the long journey back toward his father, no doubt wondering all the way how he will be received. But as soon as the father sees his son on the horizon, he rushes out to meet him.

    Jesus told this story so that we would know what God is like. He is the Father who meets us in our repentance. Put yourself in the place of *the Prodigal Son (or daughter)*. How does this encounter transform your relationship?

    _____

    _____

Now try and put yourself in the place of *an observer*—the older brother (or sister). What *questions* does this raise in your mind about the father?

_____

_____

God does not stand at a distance from us waiting until our repentance is complete. Is your relationship with your heavenly Father characterized by the transformation of an encounter with Him or by the questions of an observer?

_____

_____

8. Here are a number of applications of the seventh commandment. Read them and let them stimulate your thinking:

    a. *Baby Step: Move out of isolation and into fellowship.* The strength of your love for Christ will be the key to your triumph over sexual temptation. A new love can be stronger than an old habit. That's why the first step in overcoming the power of sexual temptation is to cultivate your love for Christ. That's why I'm convinced that most people who struggle with these temptations will find greater help by growing in their knowledge of Christ and the Word among a company of healthy believers.

    b. *Substantial Move: Fight sexual temptation.* "By the Spirit . . . *put to death* the misdeeds of the body" (Romans 8:13, emphasis added). When it comes to your battle with temptation, God does not say, "Pray about it;" He says, "Act against it." When you find impure thoughts buzzing around in your mind about that person in the office who shows an interest in you, or the adult store that you could visit on the way home, or the Internet site that was advertised on your computer, you treat these thoughts exactly like the wasp. You put the thought to death. You cut it off, give it no quarter. Swat it! If you are a Christian, you have the power to do this because the Holy Spirit lives within you. So don't listen to the Enemy when he tells you that you can't!

    c. *Radical Life-Change: Ask for God's help to embrace a spouse's repentance.* If you find that your marriage has been violated by unfaithfulness either in mind or body, the first thing you should look for from your spouse is repentance. If you do not see that, pray that it will come, and when it does, ask God to help you embrace it. If your spouse can repent, you can forgive. God's grace will make both of these things possible. And as your spouse's repentance deepens, so will your forgiveness. There are two struggles here, and the healing of the one can be the healing of the other.

How did the applications above stimulate your thinking? Write below how you would like to respond to the seventh commandment:

_____

_____

_____

chapter eight

Your Struggle

for Integrity

I. **Stealing can be defined as [trying] to get as much as possible while giving as little as possible.** When you think about the different stations on the line of stealing, which do you think are culturally acceptable and which culturally unacceptable? Circle "yes" for each that is acceptable; "no" for each that is unacceptable.

Acceptable?

yes/no   a. breaking into a home (a thief)

yes/no   b. paying your employees as little as possible (employer)

yes/no   c. giving less than full value to do the work you were hired for (employee)

yes/no   d. overpricing or doing work that is only "good enough" (cutting corners)

yes/no   e. using others' material as if it were yours (plagiarism)

yes/no   f. not paying for what you use (copying: music, software, etc.)

How might someone justify the *culturally acceptable* ones?

_____

_____

On what basis would the *culturally unacceptable* ones be considered wrong?

_____

_____

2. Remember that stealing can be defined as trying to get as much as possible while giving as little as possible. The desire to get as much as possible is *greed*. The desire to contribute as little as possible is *laziness*.

Which of the root problems (greed or laziness) do you most naturally associate with stealing? Why?

_____

_____

What does the other root problem contribute to your understanding of stealing?

_____

_____

3. If you are an employee, complete the following ranking; then proceed to item 5. If you are an employer, skip to item 4.

For employees only: Rank the following from 1 to 5 (1—the form of stealing you are *most tempted* to do and 5—the one you are *least tempted* to do).

_____a. Arriving late/leaving early/stretching lunchtime or break times

_____b. Expanding the work to be done to fill the time available

_____c. Doing the work that you like and consistently avoiding what you don't

_____d. Using work time to pursue your own projects

_____e. Engaging in evangelism or other forms of ministry during work time

Look again at the items you ranked 1 and 2. Which root problem drives these issues for you—greed or laziness? Write down any comments about this below:

_____

_____

180

4. *For employers only:* Reflect on some of the names and faces of those you employ. Ask yourself, "What is the value these workers bring to me?" Try to quantify in dollars what their work contributes to your wealth. Write your comments below:

value (in $) _____ *comments:* _____

_____

Now ask yourself, "How am I compensating these individuals?" Is it the minimum amount? Is there a gap between their value to you and your compensation of them? Write any comments below:

_____

_____

5. "You shall not steal" (Exodus 20:15). In which of the following areas have you seen family, friends, fellow students, or coworkers give in to stealing?

   ❏ "borrowing" other people's papers or speeches and pretending it's their own
   ❏ illegally copying computer software
   ❏ copying musical CDs so they don't have to buy them

What was your reaction? Did you do or say anything?

_____

_____

How do you think a Christian ought to respond in situations like these?

_____

_____

6. **We often make the mistake of creating a huge chasm in our minds between what we call "sacred" and what we call "secular."** We do this because we feel certain that God is interested in prayer, preaching, and evangelism; but we are not quite so sure that God is interested in microcircuits, school lunches, and grocery store check-outs. Write below any work you have done and the approximate years you did this:

work / years   work / years

_____ / _____-_____   _____ / _____-_____

_____ / _____-_____   _____ / _____-_____

_____ / _____-_____   _____ / _____-_____

In what ways do you think your *current* work is valuable to God?

_____

_____

7. **God has entrusted each of us with time, talent, and treasure.** You have been entrusted with the Holy Spirit and with gifts for ministry. How are you using what He has given you to contribute to the lives of others? Evaluate yourself in these three areas:

Serving others: at home/church/work; in community (using my talents)

←——————————————————————————→

how much can I get?   how much can I give?

Tithing/giving (using my possessions)

←——————————————————————————→

how much can I get?   how much can I give?

Prayer/Sabbath/work/family (using my time)

←——————————————————————————→

how much can I get?   how much can I give?

Fulfilling the eighth commandment involves a radical change of heart in which you move from being a taker to a giver. Where is your heart? Look at your evaluation of the three areas above. Place an x below to indicate overall where your heart is:

←——————————————————————————→

how much can I get?   how much can I give?

8. Let these applications of the eighth commandment stimulate your thinking:

   a. *Baby Step: Cultivate the habit of making your God-given contribution.* Wherever you go and whatever you do, you have a God-given contribution to make to the lives of other people. Cultivate the habit of looking to see how you can contribute. When you engage in a conversation or sit down for dinner with your family, try to see how you can contribute, and ask God to help you make that contribution. When you have to attend a meeting at work, look for ways in which you can contribute. Do not check out and let the conversation go on around you. There is a reason for your being there, so make your contribution.

b. *Substantial move: Begin paying back any outstanding bills or loans.* (Do you have any outstanding bills or loans? If so, what can you do to begin paying them back immediately? Contact your debtor to let him or her know of your intentions. Ask them to help you set up a plan that you can both agree on.) If you owe money on a bill and you don't pay it, that's stealing. If somebody gives you a loan and you do not repay it, that's stealing.

c. *Radical Life-Change: Learn to value your work as a good gift from God.* Do not look at work as a necessary evil that you have to endure in order to get money. View it as a God-given opportunity to contribute. Give thanks to God for giving you work and the ability to do it. (Take time each morning before you start your work, offering the work of your day directly to the Lord and give thanks to Him for this gift.) If you are employed, thank Him that somebody values what He has enabled you to do so highly that they would pay you money to do it for them.

How did the applications above stimulate your thinking? Write below how you would like to respond to the eighth commandment:

_____

_____

_____

Your Struggle

with Truth

I. Where have the effects of someone else's lies hit closest to home for you?

_____

_____

2. **The essence of lying is saying what will achieve the desired result without regard to whether it is the truth.**

Approach a trusted friend, family member, or spouse (someone who has your best interests in mind) who frequently has the opportunity to hear you talk with others. Ask him or her which of the following you most easily slip into.

The trusted person: _____

❏ **Flattering**—saying to someone's face what you would never say behind his or her back (*you want to make a good impression*)
❏ **Exaggerating**—overstating what you said, did, or accomplished, taking credit that really belongs to someone else (*you want to impress*), or overstating the wrong that was done to you (*you are looking for sympathy*)
❏ **Gossiping**—passing on news about another person that may or may not be true

Ask for a specific example (if they cannot think of one, ask another person):

_____

_____

3. Satan's first strategy was to question God's truth. "Did God really say, 'You must not eat from any tree in the garden'?" (Genesis 3:1). Can you *really* know what God has said? Undermining confidence in the Word of God set the stage for Adam and Eve's rebellion.

   If a person can't be sure about what God has said, how could he or she be expected to put it into practice? Where do your greatest areas of doubt lie in relation to the question: *Can I really know what God has said?*

   ❏ I'm not sure I can trust God (or His words).
   ❏ I'm not sure that the Bible really contains God's words (revealed by God).
   ❏ I'm not sure we can really understand the Bible (different interpretations).
   ❏ I'm not sure I can really grasp the whole Bible message (my own ability).
   ❏ I'm not sure the Bible even speaks to my life today (irrelevant).
   ❏ I'm not sure the Bible contains enough to help me (insufficient).

   What is your level of confidence in knowing what God has said?

   ⟵——————————————————————————————⟶

   very skeptical   my confidence is growing   very confident

   Why did you place yourself on the line above where you did?

   _____

   _____

4. **If we cannot know the truth, then no one can be expected to tell the truth.**

   Where do you see signs of this in our culture today?

   _____

   _____

5. "If you hold to my teaching, you are really my disciples. Then you will know the truth, and the truth will set you free" (John 8:31–32). **These are challenging words to people who have already affirmed what they believe.** Christ challenges those who say they believe to "hold" to His teaching by obeying it and putting it into practice.

When that happens, Jesus says, they will know the truth and the truth will set them free.

Reflect on this past week. Check each of the statements below that were true of you *this week,* and answer the question that follows:

❏ I affirmed a belief from God's Word.
What did you hear and affirm?

_____

❏ I held to Jesus' teachings (by putting it into practice).
What was your step of obedience?

_____

❏ I knew the truth (it became more clear and personal for me).
What became more clear and or personal?

_____

❏ The truth set me free (I experienced its power).
What were you able to do that was previously impossible for you?

_____

6. "Any group of people, whether married couples, friends, church staff, or Bible study groups, will run into serious trouble if they emphasize self-disclosure and emotional expression as premium values," writes Larry Crabb.

   What characteristics would you expect to find in a group that emphasizes self-expression over Christ-centeredness?

   _____

   _____

   What characteristics would you expect to find in a group that emphasizes Christ-centeredness over self-expression?

   _____

   _____

7. Our calling is to "speak the truth *in love*" (Ephesians 4:15, emphasis added). That means that I am to speak the truth in a way that will be in the best interests of the hearer.

So there will be times when I have to exercise courage and say what someone does not want to hear (confront), **and there will be other times when I have to exercise restraint and hold back what a person is not ready to hear** (conceal). Which of these is most difficult for you? Why?

_____

_____

8. Here are some applications of the ninth commandment for you to consider:

a. *Baby Step: Take a step of personal obedience this week.* When you take a step of obedience, Jesus promises that two things will happen. First, "you will know the truth." What seemed cloudy and distant will become clear and personal. It will be in you, and it will be true for you. Second, "the truth will set you free." Things that bound you will bind you no longer. Things that you could not do before will become possible for you.

b. *Substantial Move: Stop flattering, exaggerating, or gossiping.* (See your notes from question #2.) The reason we are prone to lying is that we are more deeply committed to ourselves than we are committed to the truth. Truth is hard for sinners because it never puts us in a pure light. We like to think of ourselves as seekers after truth. In reality, our first instinct is to run from it.

c. *Radical Life-Change: Practice speaking the truth in love.* "Do not let any unwholesome talk come out of your mouths, but only what is helpful for building others up according to their needs, that it may benefit those who listen" (Ephesians 4:29). Learn to weigh the effects of what you say in the light of the trust you have earned.

How did the applications above stimulate your thinking? Write below how you would like to respond to the ninth commandment:

_____

_____

chapter ten

Your Struggle
for Contentment

I. When do you most notice your own struggle with contentment?

_____

_____

2. **The problem for morally upright people . . . is that they find it very difficult to feel that they need a Savior.** How do you feel about your own religious life?

←————————————————————————————→

I feel my need of a Savior   I feel my need *and* believe   I feel like I am a
                       I'm a pretty good person   pretty good person

How do you think a person's moral life affects his or her need for a Savior?

_____

_____

3. More than that, he is a true believer in God, he knows that beyond death lies eternity, and he wants to make sure that he is ready. **So he has set the goal of living a good life:** He attends church, he prays to God, and he gives generously to good causes.

Place a check in the box next to *the good life* you share with him:

❏ You are a true believer in God.
❏ You know that beyond death lies eternity.
❏ You attend church.
❏ You pray to God.
❏ You give generously to good causes.

Based on your answers above, how *good* of a *life* have you lived?

not so good _____   *pretty* good _____   *very* good, indeed! _____

4. **There are many reasons why people live a moral life that have little or nothing to do with loving God or neighbor.**

    Think back over your last week and identify three moral decisions you made:

    1. _____ primary: _____ secondary: _____
    2. _____ primary: _____ secondary: _____
    3. _____ primary: _____ secondary: _____

    Place the abbreviation from below next to the decision above, indicating the primary and secondary reasons (if you can identify them) for your behavior:

    The peer factor—PF (We all know that a large part of our behavior will reflect the behavior of [our] friends.)

    The fear factor—FF (Sometimes the reason that we do not steal, lie, or commit adultery has to do with the fear of the consequences.)

    A deep love for God—DL (Your thoughts reveal the real condition of your heart.)

    Was there a time this week when you wrongly assumed that doing "the right thing" was evidence of your love for God? If so, explain:

    _____

    _____

5. "I would not have known what sin was except through the law" (Romans 7:7). For many years, Paul had looked at the commandments and concluded that he was morally upright. Now he tells us that the commandments showed him that he was a sinner. What made the difference?

    The answer is the tenth commandment. "I would not have known what it was to covet if the law had not said 'Do not covet.'"

(Romans 7:7). **It strangled the life out of my self-righteousness.** How is your self-righteousness?

strangled! _____   limping along _____   alive and well! _____
(by the tenth   (wounded by the   (unscathed by the
commandment)   tenth commandment)   tenth commandment)

6. There are many ways to change a person's behavior. If all you want to do is to stop drinking or break free from some other compulsive habit, you don't need Jesus to do that. You can do it with some good therapy, accountability, and an effective support group.

    There are many ways to deal with the symptoms, but only Christ can deal with the disease. Do you agree/disagree with this statement? Why or why not?

    _____

    _____

7. **Their idea of Christianity is that we do our best to follow the Law and ask for forgiveness when we fail to live up to this standard.** The gospel is more than forgiveness and the Law. When you come to faith in Jesus Christ, God puts His Spirit within you. That's His promise. "I will give you *a new heart* and put *a new spirit* in you. . . . *I will put my Spirit in you* and move you to follow my decrees and be careful to keep my laws" (Ezekiel 36:26–27, emphasis added).

    What is the *difference in expectations* between these two views of Christianity?

    _____

    _____

8. Consider these applications of the tenth commandment:

    a. *Baby Step: Take your cues from Christ through repentance and faith.* Peer factor morality doesn't bring you any closer to God because it does not arise from love but from conforming to what everyone else is doing. God calls us not just to do right but to be right, and that means He is looking for something deeper than actions that reflect the behavior of other people around us.

b. *Substantial Move: Take up a new battle strategy: fighting against sin.* Sin is not merely a matter of actions and deeds; it is something within the heart that leads to the action. Sins are nothing but the symptoms of a disease called sin, and it is not the symptoms that matter but the disease, for it is the disease that kills, not the symptoms. (See also Psalm 51.)

c. *Radical Life-Change: Reevaluate your position before God.* The apostle Paul saw the hollowness of his own morality. He embraced the tough message of his failure before God's Law. That led him to Christ and to a new life.

How did the applications above stimulate your thinking? Write below how you would like to respond to the tenth commandment:

_____

_____

_____

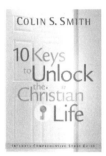

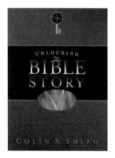